STATE, SOCIETY & DEMOCRACY IN MOROCCO
The Limits of Associative Life

Azzedine Layachi

مركز الدراسات العربية المعاصرة ـ جامعة جورجتاون

CENTER FOR CONTEMPORARY ARAB STUDIES
Edmund A. Walsh School of Foreign Service
Georgetown University

THE CENTER FOR CONTEMPORARY ARAB STUDIES at Georgetown University was founded in 1975 to enlarge and enrich academic studies and scholarly research on the Arab world. CCAS is the only academic institution in the United States devoted solely to the study of the contemporary Arab world. It administers a Master's degree program in Arab Studies as well as graduate and undergraduate certificate programs.

CCAS sponsors numerous public events, the highlight of which is an annual symposium on a topic of contemporary importance to the region, and an annual distinguished lecture in Arab Studies. The Center's Community Resource Service has assisted hundreds of secondary school teachers through twice annual workshops providing information and instructional materials on the Arab world. The Center's publication program has published more than fifty books and papers on contemporary issues in the Arab world.

ISBN 0-932568-25-4
Library of Congress Catalog Card Number: 98-73092

STATE, SOCIETY & DEMOCRACY IN MOROCCO
The Limits of Associative Life

Contents

State, Society, and Democracy in Morocco

Acknowledgment

This work would not have been completed without the support and assistance of various individuals and institutions. I am grateful for the financial support of the American Institute of Maghrebi Studies in Los Angeles, and the Summer Research Support Program of St. John's University. Warm thanks go to the Moroccan-American Commission for Educational and Cultural Cooperation (Fulbright office) in Rabat, especially former Director Ed Thomas and his diligent assistant Saadia Mask; their help was beyond my expectations.

Many thanks go also to the Center for Contemporary Arab Studies at Georgetown University, especially Publications Coordinator Maggy Zanger for her diligent and conscientious work on the manuscript, and the editorial assistance of Martha Wenger.

I would like to thank also the Moroccan friends and colleagues who provided me with their generous assistance and guidance during my search for civil society in their country, particularly Abdesselam Cheddadi and Abdallah Saaf of the Mohamed V University in Rabat. Among the many new friends that I made during my research in Morocco, special thanks go to those who where particularly helpful in many ways, even if only by their moral support and the time they spent with me debating issues pertaining to my research. They are Khadija Khai, Mohamed and Fatma-Zohra Medjati Alam, Said Temsamani, and Fatma Ezzahra El-Hatimi.

I thank my wife, Rachida whose encouragement (and pressure, at times) helped me finish the writing of this manuscript.

Introduction

A multitude of internal and external factors have recently caused major domestic changes across the Maghrib and the Mashriq. These factors of change are so intricate and powerful that the best thing political leaders have been able to do, short of leaving power to new societal forces, has been to try to control the pace of unavoidable change. The Hegelian state may be unworkable nowadays, but the specter of de Tocqueville's civil society seems to haunt even the most conservative states and the most authoritarian rulers in the region.

The issue of state-society relations has recently imposed itself upon the Arab world as new realities and social forces challenge state institutions, power arrangements, and leaders. Some leaders have lost legitimacy; some have lagged behind in their response to changing times. Algeria, Tunisia, and Egypt represent the most critical examples of state-society friction between new realities and old methods of governance, between new types of problems and obsolete institutional responses, and between new sectors of society and old power structures. Some regimes have managed to steer their societies away from the point of rupture, but that may only be a temporary respite if major social, economic, and political adjustments are not urgently undertaken. State-society relations must be redefined in ways that incorporate important societal groups in the developmental experience and heed calls for inclusive and participatory political and economic processes.

Morocco has experienced some of the major changes that have swept the Arab world in recent years. It has managed to maintain relative stability and social peace in spite of grave social and economic difficulties and minimal progress toward redefining state-society relations. This country presents a peculiar mixture of relative political pluralism and flexible authoritarianism; it has a system that rests on the centrality of the king and the explicit acceptance by the opposition of his legitimacy and power. This arrangement precludes, *a priori*, the very existence of social and political forces that could challenge such centrality, although Moroccan intellectuals, politicians, and businessmen have begun to realize that a peaceful evolution for the country will require the institutionalization of "civil society," both as a process and as a system of representation and articulation of societal interests.

Morocco constitutes an interesting case study mostly because of two paradoxes it presents. The first paradox is the absence of a civil society—as defined below—in spite of the perennial existence of an associative life. The second is the relative political stability Morocco has enjoyed for more than two decades despite grave social and economic problems.

These paradoxes are analyzed here through the examination of the role of independently mobilized societal forces in Morocco. Several questions are tackled: Is "civil society" a useful analytical notion for this case? Can it ever be a social and political practice in Morocco? Why has Morocco's long experience with political pluralism not given birth to a viable and vibrant civil society that could limit the over-extension of the powers of the state and the monarchy? Is democratization feasible in the context of Morocco's current power structure and socio-political reality? Will the Moroccan state withstand the political liberalization that may result from the economic changes of structural adjustment?

This work focuses thus on the nature and place of civil society in Moroccan political, economic, and cultural spheres, i.e., the role of independently mobilized social forces in the process of making binding decisions "for the whole society." Because of difficulties encountered when applying to Morocco the notion of civil society as an analytical and explanatory tool, this study rests on the notion and practice of political power and stems from the belief that state-society relations are power relations that evolve around deciding "who gets what, when, and how."

This study of Morocco was inspired by questions about the notion of civil society, about its relation to the idea of the state, and about the theoretical and empirical usefulness of both constructs. The first section of this book examines the theoretical and philosophical underpinnings of the concept of civil society and state in an effort to sort out the contributions made by various thinkers to our understanding of these abstract elements. A working definition of civil society is presented, along with definitions of democratization and political liberalization.

The empirical background to the case study is set out in two sections on Morocco's economic and social evolution over the last 30 years, as well as on the nature of the state and regime in place. International factors perceived to have affected the recent economic and political evolution of Morocco are examined in the next section, with particular attention paid to their contribution to the promotion or inhibition of the development of civil society and democracy. The subsequent three sections analyze the relationship between associative life and civil society in Morocco and examine the nature and role of the press and some of the more important civic associations and political parties. These sections end with a discussion of the 1993 and 1997 elections and the new constitutional arrangement established by the 1996 referendum and by the parliamentary vote of 1997. The next section looks into the prospects for civil society and democracy in Morocco in light of the findings of this research and of the most recent developments in the country. The book concludes with a set of analytical results and normative propositions.

1

State, Civil Society and Democratization

The concept of state has generated scholarship for centuries, yet there is no generally agreed upon understanding of it. The same can be said about the notion of civil society. Both have recently returned to the forefront as scholars and politicians engaged in frantic efforts to understand the rapid changes since the late 1980s in the Third World, Eastern Europe, and former Soviet republics. Social scientists in general, and political scientists in particular, have found themselves lacking adequate theoretical frameworks and conceptual tools to understand unexpected events such as the fall of the communist states or the rise of political Islam. Observers and scholars find themselves ill-equipped to predict even short-term developments.

Because of the lack of new and refreshing perspectives, some outmoded theories were revisited in the late 1980s and early 1990s. Among the revived theoretical tools is the notion of civil society,[1] which was taken directly from the semi-retired modernization school of the 1960s. Since neither the authoritarian model nor the modernization school offered satisfactory explanations for the persistence of autocratic regimes and religious revivalism in seemingly modernizing societies, the concept of state and the notion of civil society were exhumed and refurbished to serve as tools to explain change, as well as to promote development in a given direction. However, some writings focused on the nature of the state and promoted a model for the future based almost exclusively on its reform,[2] while others emphasized change through the promotion of civil society.[3] In this book, empirical and theoretical separation is replaced with a more dynamic perspective which links the notions of state and civil society in the analysis of current empirical situations.

The State

The Hegelian definition of the state includes the entire political community which pursues national or universal objectives through a central government or a supreme public authority.[4] For Hegel, there seems to be no distinction between state and society. When there is a highly developed civil society, state and society are conflate into a whole called the "ethical community,"[5] which seems to be endowed by Hegel with "something that transcends the mere use of force or the power to coerce. The state. . . is a mode of relating which stresses shared values and common sacrifices at the expense of individual interests."[6]

Karl Marx viewed the state as directly linked to the capitalist mode of production and not as an autonomous entity. While recognizing the possibility of some historical moments where the state may be autonomous, Marx viewed it as "organized power" in the hands of one class which uses it to oppress another one. Whether in capitalism or in socialism, the state is in the hands of the dominant class, organized as the ruling class.[7]

For Max Weber, the state resulted directly from rationalization and specialization in Western capitalist societies.[8] Contrary to Karl Marx and Friedrich Engels, however, Weber did not believe the state had an organic link to a given social or economic class. He defined it in terms of rationality and legitimate authority, and attributed to it the monopoly use of force and coercion.

Nowadays, a restrictive definition of the state tends to include "all those individuals who occupy offices that authorize them, and them alone, to make and apply decisions that are binding upon any part and all parts of a territorially circumscribed population."[9] This definition by Eric Nordlinger emphasizes the human content of the state and is thus relevant to many cases. The state acquires a tangible meaning when it is identified through the individuals who run its institutions. Rejecting any separation between state and society, Timothy Mitchell adds that we should think of the state "not as an actual structure but as the powerful, metaphysical effect of practices that make such structures appear to exist."[10]

To what extent do these conceptualizations of the state help us understand what is happening today in parts of the Arab world, and in Morocco in particular? In the case of Morocco where state and society interpenetrate in various forms and at many levels, can the liberal distinction between state and society be useful as an explanatory tool?

For the limited purpose of this book, a working definition of the state includes not only territoriality, population, and government, but also decision-making institutions and processes, as well as identifiable individual decision makers. As a sovereign authority, the state also constitutes an accepted focus of identity. The conceptualizations of the state outlined above can serve at best only as guides in the study of modern Arab states, notably because these states came into existence in a particular fashion and acquired a nature that is quite different from that of Western liberal states. In the case of Morocco, as will be shown, the concept of *makhzen*—an informal source of authority— may be a more useful notion for explaining the nature of the Moroccan state and for understanding those embedded characteristics that have prevented its transformation into a modern structure capable of handling the demands of society. The same reservations can be expressed about the notion of civil society—a notion that has become popular among scholars searching for an explanation for dramatic change in several parts of the world.

Civil Society

Hegel was one of the first scholars to examine civil society and its relationship with the state. For him, civil society is a set of private individuals, classes, groups, and institutions whose actions are independent from the state but who are regulated by civil law. "[C]ivil society . . . is conceived not as a natural condition of freedom but as a *historically produced* sphere of ethical life... positioned between the simple world of the patriarchal household and the universal state. "The market economy, social classes, corporations, and the institutions which manage the 'welfare'... and civil law are its constitutive elements.[11] Hegel concluded his analysis with the proposition that, because of its diverse composition (often with conflicting interests), civil society can be "civil" only if it is "ordered politically," i.e., subjected to the "higher surveillance of the state." Therefore, civil society can exist only under the control of a "supervising strong state." Civil society is necessary but subordinate to a universal political community.

Another early thinker who used this notion, John Locke, defined civil society in opposition to the state of nature. For him, "the end of civil society [is] to avoid and remedy those inconveniences of the state of nature...." It meant a political society that rests on a social contract between rational men enjoying civil liberties.[12]

Alexis de Tocqueville viewed civil society as "the independent eye of society," an eye made up of a plurality of self-organized and vigilant civil associations. An independent and autonomous civil society is necessary for the consolidation of democracy, de Tocqueville believed, and without it, nothing will prevent those in power from becoming dictators.[13]

The notion of civil society has a entirely different meaning for Marxists. In *The German Ideology*, Karl Marx and Friedrich Engels give civil society an economic content. For them, it includes "all the material relations of individuals within a definite stage of the development of productive forces." It constitutes "the whole commercial and industrial life of a given stage and, insofar, transcends the state and the nation, though, on the other hand again, it must assert itself in its foreign relations as a nationality, and inwardly must organize itself as state."[14] State and civil society are linked in capitalism by the fact that the dominant social class uses the state as an instrument to assert itself domestically and internationally.

Antonio Gramsci looked for civil society not in infrastructure, as Marx did, but in the superstructural sphere. For Gramsci, the superstructure consists of a civil society, that is, all private organizations, including the political society, i.e., the state. Whereas for Marx, civil society encompasses economic relations, for Gramsci it comprises all ideological and cultural interactions. According to Gramsci, civil society constitutes the political and cultural hegemony that a social group exercises over the whole society; in his words, "the ethical content of the state."[15] The most important conclusion Gramsci draws from this proposition is that civil society would be the place where other social groups and classes can undermine the position of the bourgeoisie and prepare for revolution against the capitalist state. Gramsci viewed civil society as a way of "conceptually analyzing existing and emerging empirical relations between social and political forces and their organizational (structural) and ideological (superstructural) manifestations." He also saw it as "a 'pragmatic' analysis seeking to formulate a political strategy or action program for the 'progressive' forces in civil society, the 'new historic bloc'."[16] Some scholars saw in the Polish experience of the 1980s the realization of the Gramscian civil society—a successful strategy orchestrated by the labor movement Solidarity to unseat the dominant party-state.

Drawing from these various theoretical positions and from empirical evidence, I suggest that civil society be understood as a set of social, economic, cultural, and political groupings, distinct and independent from the state, that perform functions of aggregation and articulation of particular interests, and seeks either to influence state decisions or to capture the state itself. In the political sphere, civil society checks state arbitrariness while serving as a buffer between state power and private spheres. Finally, civil society is an independent process of mobilization of various interests for change or for the maintenance of the status quo.

In recent studies of change in the Third World in general, and in the Arab world in particular, civil society has slowly become a key notion.[17] Society's recent intervention in the political arena of North African countries such as Algeria and Tunisia and in other areas of the Middle East such as the West Bank, Jordan, and Egypt indicates what may be the start of a serious erosion of the overwhelming state control of the political domain, as well as the beginning of a rethinking of state-society relations in many developing countries.[18]

To a number of scholars and political observers this development reflects, almost automatically, the rise of civil society and the beginning of the retreat of the authoritarian state in many countries of the Third World.[19] This research has found, however, that this is not verified in Morocco, where associative life has not been an automatic indication of the existence of civil society.

Democratization

The notion of democratization is often used to refer to a process that is not well understood and is, in fact, more complex and uncertain than usually thought. Democratization is not democracy itself, but rather a long and arduous process that may lead either to democracy or to a reverse movement toward authoritarianism (as, for example, in Tunisia and Russia), to chaos (as in Zaire and Somalia), or to a vicious internal conflict within a polarized society (as in Algeria).

For our purpose here, "democratization" is understood as a process whereby state control over society is slowly diminished to a point where the state becomes less arbitrary and more prone to bargaining with the most representative groups of the social, economic, and cultural spheres. With democratization, the state would resort less to a command type of governance and more to negotiated public policies. Democratization may strengthen the state's legitimacy. The state is expected to remain the most important institution, while society acquires greater autonomy and is allowed, through independently organized and mobilized societal interests, more access to policy making. According to Philippe Schmitter and Guillermo O'Donnell, democratization is to be preceded by "political liberalization" which would allow for political freedoms and establish safeguards against the arbitrary action of the state.[20] Following political liberalization, the democratization process would have to instill among both the rulers and the ruled a political culture which allows for tolerance of opposing views and beliefs and promotes political bargaining and compromise. In Morocco, as in most Arab countries, many of these elements are absent, and when a few of them are sometimes exhibited or rhetorically promoted, it is often because the traditional sources of strength and legitimacy of the regime have failed.

In the case of Morocco, traditional forms of legitimation and mobilization have weakened over the years and new ones have slowly taken shape. These new forms, however, have not yet been accompanied by genuine political liberalization and democratization. While several existing domestic and international ingredients constitute today forceful pressures for democratic change, many other factors mitigate against such a prospect.

Notes

1. Richard Norton, ed., *Civil Society in the Middle East* (Netherlands: E. J. Brill, 1994).

2. I. William Zartman, ed., *Collapsed States: The Disintegration and Restoration of Legitimate Authority* (Boulder, CO: Lynne Rienner, 1995). This collection of works focuses on the collapse of states and public authority in Africa.

3. The concept of state as an analytical and normative instrument was pushed aside by the society-centered perspective which emphasizes societal dynamics and forces as primary agents of change. The society-centered perspective of the 1970s (e.g., the neo-Marxists) viewed the state as a dependent variable affected by several societal factors. The concept of state as an autonomous agent was revived in the 1980s in a series of writings. For a good review of this state-centered literature, see Theda Skocpol, "Bringing the State Back In," in Peter B. Evens, Dietrich Rueschemeyer, and Theda Skocpol, *Bringing the State Back In* (Cambridge: Cambridge University Press, 1985); and Stephen Krasner, "Approaches to the State: Alternative Conceptions and Historical Dynamics,"

Comparative Politics 16:2, 1984.

4. Zbigniew A. Pelczynski, "Solidarity and the 'Rebirth of Civil Society' in Poland," in John Keane, ed., *Civil Society and the State: New European Perspectives* (New York: Verso, 1988), p. 364. See also Zbigniew A. Pelczynski, ed., *The State and Civil Society: Studies in Hegel's Political Philosophy* (Cambridge: Cambridge University Press, 1984).

5. G. W. Hegel, *Philosophy of Right* (Oxford: Oxford University Press, 1952), p. 132.

6. Steven B. Smith, "Hegel's View on War, the State and International Relations," *The American Political Science Review* 77:3, September 1983, p. 625.

7. Karl Marx, "Manifesto of the Communist Party," in Karl Marx and Friedrich Engels, *Selected Works* (New York: International Publishers, 1968), pp. 35-63.

8. Max Weber, *The Protestant Ethic and the Spirit of Capitalism* (New York: Charles Scribner's Sons, 1958).

9. Eric Nordlinger, *On the Autonomy of the Democratic State* (Cambridge, MA: Harvard University Press, 1981), p. 362.

10. Timothy Mitchell, "The Limits of the State: Beyond Statist Approaches and Their Critics," in *The American Political Science Review* 85:1, March 1991, pp. 77-96, cited in René Lemarchand, "Uncivil States and Civil Societies: How Illusion Became Reality," *Journal of Modern African Studies* 30:2, 1992, p. 180.

11. John Keane, "Despotism and Democracy: The Origins of the Distinction between Civil Society and the State," in John Keane, ed., *Civil Society and the State: New European Perspectives* (New York: Verso, 1988), p. 50.

12. John Locke, *The Second Treaties on Civil Government*, 1690 (New York: Prometheus Books, 1986), pp. 44-50.

13. Alexis de Tocqueville, *Democracy in America* (New York: Langley, 1845).

14. Karl Marx and Friedrich Engels, "The German Ideology," in Richard T. Garner and Andrew Oldenquist, eds., *Society and the Individual: Readings in Political and Social Philosophy* (Belmont, CA: Wadsworth, 1990), p. 219.

15. Antonio Gramsci, *Past and Present* (1966), p. 164, cited in Norberto Bobbio, "Gramsci and the Concept of Civil Society," in John Keane, ed., *Civil Society and the State* (New York: Verso, 1988), p. 84.

16. Pelczynski, "Solidarity," op. cit., p. 371.

17. For an overview of the concept of civil society in political and academic discourse in the Arab world, see Mustapha Kamel al-Sayyid, "The Concept of Civil Society and the Arab World," in Rex Brynen, Bahgat Korany, and Paul Noble, eds., *Political Liberalization and Democratization in the Arab World, Volume 1: Theoretical Perspectives* (Boulder, CO: Lynne Rienner, 1995), pp. 131-147. See also the proceedings of the first study solicited by the Arab League's Center for Arab Unity Studies, *al-Moujtama'a al-Madani fi al-Watan al-Arabi wa Dawruhu fi Tahkik al-Dimukrattiyya* [Civil Society in the Arab World and its Role in Democratic Change] (Beirut, Lebanon: Center for Arab Union Studies, 1992).

18. Azzedine Layachi, "Reinstating the State or Instating Civil Society: The Dilemma of Algeria's Transition," in Zartman, *Collapsed States,* op. cit., p. 172.

19. This view is reflected and defended in the writings of Richard Norton and his Civil Society Project and also in the program on Arab Civil Society developed by the Ibn Khaldoun Center for Development Studies, Cairo, Egypt.

20. Guillermo O'Donnell and Philippe C. Schmitter, *Transitions from Authoritarian Rule: Tentative Conclusions about Uncertain Democracies* (Baltimore, MD: Johns Hopkins University Press, 1986), cited in Michel Camau, "Changes of Regimes in the Maghreb: The Hazards of Democratization," paper presented at the 1990 Annual Meeting of the Middle East Studies Association (MESA), p. 5.

II

The Economy and Society

L ocated on the westernmost part of North Africa just twelve miles south of Europe, Morocco occupies a strategic location that controls the lower half of the Strait of Gibraltar on the Mediterranean Sea, while enjoying a long coastline on the Atlantic Ocean. Bordered on the east by Algeria, and on the south by the Western Sahara,[1] Morocco covers 172,419 square miles and has a population of 27 million people which increases by 2 percent every year.[2] The official language is Arabic, but Tamazight (Berber) and French are widely used as well. Ethnically, Morocco is a mix of Arabs and Imazighen (Berbers), with the Tamazight-speaking minority making up 40 percent.[3] Islam is the religion of nearly all of the population.

Morocco has a free-market economy with large governmental participation, though the role of government is curtailed now by a sweeping privatization program. King Hassan II, however, still makes or approves most important economic decisions.

With a per capita gross national product of $1,110 in 1995 (up from $960 in 1990),[4] Morocco belongs to the lower middle-income countries of the world. It holds 75 percent of world phosphate reserves and is the largest exporter of that commodity. The country also exports foodstuffs but has a traditional agricultural sector. Morocco also has some of the richest fishing waters in the world, a sophisticated tourist industry, and a small manufacturing sector. Remittances from Moroccans working abroad bring in $2.5 billion a year. The emigrant workforce, which is mostly in Europe, constitutes 5 percent of the total Moroccan population and approximately 10 percent of the national workforce.[5]

The 1975 annexation of the Western Sahara following the withdrawal of the Spanish colonialists cost Morocco close to $1 billion a year during the irredentist campaign of the late 1970s and much of the 1980s. Even though much of that money was provided by Saudi Arabia,

Morocco's economic performance has suffered tremendously. During those years, the war was costing Morocco close to 45 percent of its annual budget.[6] An economic crunch due to the war efforts coupled with a fall in commodity prices, an alarming balance of trade deficit, and a high foreign debt compelled the king to impose in 1978 an economic stabilization program and to agree in 1983 to an IMF sponsored structural adjustment program (known in Morocco by its French acronym PAS). When the first economic restructuring measures were implemented in the 1980s under the IMF program, they generated riots and violence throughout the kingdom. In the early 1990s, there was additional unrest and the gap between a rich minority and a poor majority continued to widen. Data published by the United Nations Development Program indicate, for example, that the income share of the lowest 40 percent of households has gone down from 22.8 percent of total income in 1981 to 17.1 percent in 1992, even though the GNP per capita increased from $960 to $1,050 between 1990 and 1992.[7]

Based on map from *Religion and Power in Morocco*, Henry Munson, Jr. (Yale University Press).

Structural Adjustment and its Impact

Following the self-imposed stabilization programs of 1978 and 1981 that failed to produce the expected economic results, Morocco agreed to an IMF and World Bank sponsored structural adjustment program that lasted from 1983 to 1992. The primary purpose of structural adjustment was to bring about economic growth through a market economy that encourages private investment, diminishes state economic involvement, liberalizes commerce, entices foreign investment, and promotes exports. Morocco would not have been able to engage in this relatively aggressive structural adjustment without the help of international institutions and multilateral debt relief agreements (seven between 1980 and 1991). The adjustment program came, however, with a heavy social cost and an important political risk. By 1990, real wages had fallen dramatically, unemployment had risen, and inflation, albeit relatively controlled, constituted a problem for fixed incomes.[8] Several street riots shook the country in the 1980s and 1990s, each followed by massive repression that left many people dead.

However, after 10 years of intense economic restructuring, the aggregate economic outlook of Morocco improved relatively as privatization has gained momentum, and some foreign businesses have been enticed by generous investment regulations. Between 1985 and 1995, Morocco's budget deficit declined from 12 percent to 3 percent of the GDP, exports increased by 9.7 percent, the debt-to-GDP ratio fell from 123 percent to 81 percent, and the debt-servicing ratio (relative to export earning) fell from a high 70 percent to 33 percent, but constituted in 1995 the biggest expenditure item in the budget at 27.67 billion dirhams ($3.11 billion), up slightly from 1994.[9] By 1995, the foreign debt reached $22.14, up from $20.66 billion in 1993 and $8.47 billion in 1980.[10]

Reversing somewhat the 1970s wave of "Morocconization," which required a Moroccan majority ownership in many businesses, the structural adjustment program called for opening the economy to foreign investors through large-scale privatization and a meaningful retreat of the state from most economic activities. Despite much publicity, however, the pace of privatization of state-owned enterprises did not pick up until 1994. The companies put up for privatization included even those in "strategic" industries such as oil, petrochemicals, transportation, and communications, which had always been controlled by the state. By mid-1995, though, not one quarter of the corporations to be privatized had been sold. It was planned that before the end of the year, the state companies to be privatized would include three in agriculture, 14 in the food sector, 12 in textiles and leather, 18 in other areas of industrial production, nine in the banking and financial sector, 38 in tourism, and 18 in other services. In spite of various difficulties, the Moroccan state managed to sell two of its most important concerns: the Societé Nationale d'Investissement (National Investment Company) was sold at the end of 1994, and the Banque Marocaine du Commerce Extérieur (Moroccan Bank of Foreign Trade) was privatized in early 1995. The buyers included national and foreign businesses and individuals. The pace of privatization has been hampered by various factors, including smuggling, tax evasion, government corruption, slow and limited market deregulation, improper corporate audits, lack of domestic skilled management, and unequal infrastructural development among regions.

Regional Economic Integration: the UMA or the EU?

In 1989, the fragile hope of developing a North African common market was placed in the hands of the Arab Maghreb Union (known by its French acronym UMA) which joined Algeria, Libya, Mauritania, Morocco, and Tunisia. The UMA is still in the process of establishing regional structures for cooperation among its member countries, all of which (especially Morocco) suddenly faced important commercial losses when the European countries diminished their agricultural imports from the North African region. This happened after the European Economic Community (now the European Union) moved toward greater economic integration.

Major internal and regional political problems led some Moroccan officials to believe that Maghribi economic integration would not alleviate their country's economic and social difficulties. The prospects for regional integration became even more remote in the context of the violent Islamist rebellion in Algeria which began in 1991, and after Morocco reinstated travel visas for Algerians in August 1994. Morocco's visa decision was prompted by an armed attack which killed two Spanish tourists in a luxury hotel of Marrakesh; the attack was attributed to French Islamists of Algerian descent. Algeria responded by closing the border with its western neighbor. Except for a major gas pipeline that has linked Algeria with Europe via Morocco since the end of 1996,

Morocco's economic exchanges with its Maghribi partners have remained limited (less than 10 percent of all foreign commercial exchanges); 60 percent of all Maghribi foreign business is conducted with Europe. It is thus no surprise that some Moroccans, starting with King Hassan himself, believe that Morocco's economic well-being is better guaranteed by a close association with France or Spain or with the European Union (EU), than with its North African neighbors.

In 1987 Morocco applied for membership in what is now the EU, but was turned down. In 1995, however, the EU agreed to establish a special relationship with the North African kingdom, which includes, among other things, membership in a free-trading zone. The Moroccan application for membership in the EU was supported by the argument that more than half of Morocco's trade was with the EU and that the country had a liberal economic system and a multiparty democracy. The best Morocco has been able to obtain from the Europeans is membership in a free-trading zone and three 1988 agreements regarding closer association with the EEC, financial aid, and fishing in Moroccan territorial waters. The prospects of realizing a much closer association with the EU are dim for now, and Morocco's trade deficit with Europe is expected to continue to rise.

It is important to note that there exists among the Moroccan political elite an opposition to close association with the EU. Such opposition is encountered mostly on the left (e.g., the party of the Socialist Union of Popular Forces and the Confederation of Labor) which believes that Morocco's economic prosperity should be sought in the Maghrib and that Europe offers only consumer products, not jobs and equal business opportunities.[11]

Development Prospects

By mid-1995, the short-term economic outlook in most sectors did not appear very good for Morocco. Agricultural production, which provides 25 percent of export earnings and employs 40 percent of the workforce, had been particularly disastrous, following a long, severe drought. The 1995 crops amounted to only one quarter of a normal year's harvest. Only phosphate mining remained strong relative to the poorer performance of most other sectors, including tourism, which is the country's third largest source of hard currency after phosphates exports and remittances from abroad. Moreover, general unemployment rose to a point where more than 170,000 university graduates are today without jobs.

Since the beginning of the structural adjustment program in 1983, Morocco has been trying hard to attract foreign investors to compensate for a shortage of domestic capital, and to use international corporations as a gateway to foreign markets, notably Europe. Even though the country has been relatively attractive to foreign investors because of its proximity to Europe, its skilled workers, and its fairly well-developed infrastructure, the influx of foreign capital that was expected did not take place. Reasons for lagging investment include a slow bureaucracy, corruption, and a judicial system that is not protective of foreign business interests.

Recent studies of Morocco predict that the country's economic and demographic crisis may worsen in the short-term. Even though Morocco has had a relatively low population growth rate for a developing country — less than 2 percent — the current economic transformations will have a hard time meeting the rising demands for employment and services. Most of these demands come from urban centers, especially Rabat, Salé, and Casablanca, which alone comprise 40 percent of the urban population. The rural areas remain characterized by lower standards of living for the vast majority and acute inequality in land ownership and income distribution: "75 percent of rural households own less than two hectares each and account for only 16 percent of all arable land; approximately 30 percent of rural households have no land at all or extremely small parcels."[12] Government policies benefit mostly the modern, export-oriented sectors controlled by a handful of landowners and businesses. Economic policies favor the expansion of Moroccan capital, especially in the textile and leather industries, and encourage Moroccans to participate in joint ventures with foreign capital, mostly in food processing and tourism.

Morocco's restructuring efforts have been substantial, but have not, so far, translated into tangible improvements in the living standards of most of society. The aggressive policy of economic restructuring for the purposes of reorienting development and guaranteeing a better place for the country in the global economy carries political and social costs which may constitute serious obstacles to growth and development. Morocco remains a poor and underdeveloped country characterized by gross income disparities across social classes and regions and also between urban and rural populations. A new class of urban bourgeoisie has developed in recent decades while the urban poor have been further pauperized with fewer and fewer opportunities for employment at home and abroad. This situation has created a dangerous concentration of desperately poor people in overgrown cities such as Casablanca, Fez, Tangier, Marrakesh, Rabat, and Salé.

If the current policy of transforming the Moroccan economy into a diversified export-oriented one keeps enriching the business and state elite without improving the plight of the poor, radical challenges from various disaffected groups may put the regime at risk, especially if the disaffected and poor are mobilized by an organized, politicized Islam. To increase the living standards of its poor majority, Morocco's shift to an export-oriented and increasingly privatized economy must lead to sustained growth and a more equitable distribution of income and opportunities.

Notes

1. The fate of the Western Sahara (the territory south of Morocco) is expected to be decided by a referendum organized by the United Nations. This vote was postponed several times because of disagreement between the Saharawi liberation movement, the Polisario Front, and Morocco, which has already annexed most of the territory.

2. The World Bank, *World Development Report 1997* (New York: Oxford University Press, 1997).

3. It should be noted that several militant Amazigh (Berber) movements in Algeria and Morocco claim that the whole of the Maghrib is in essence Berber and that Arabs and Arabic culture constitute a minor characteristic of the region. These movements prefer that "Berbers" be referred to as Imazighen and their language as Tamazight.

4. The World Bank, *World Development Report 1997*, op. cit.

5. Youssef Courbage, "Demographic Change in the Arab World: The Impact of Migration, Education and Taxes in Egypt and Morocco," *Middle East Report* 190, September-October 1994, p. 21.

6. John Damis, "Morocco and the Western Sahara," *Current History,* April 1990, p. 166. See also Daniel Volman, "The Role of Military Assistance in the Western Sahara War," in Yahia H. Zoubir and Daniel Volman, eds., *International Dimensions of the Western Sahara Conflict* (Westport, CT: Praeger, 1993), pp.151-168; Mark A. Tessler, John P. Entelis, and Gregory W. White, "Kingdom of Morocco," in David E. Long and Bernard Reich, eds., *The Government and Politics of the Middle East and North Africa* (Boulder, CO: Westview Press, 1995), p. 376.

7. United Nations Development Program, *Human Development Report 1993* (New York: Oxford University Press, 1993), and UNDP, *Human Development Report 1995.*

8. For a comparative analysis of Morocco's structural adjustment policies, see Karen Pfeifer, "Between Rocks and Hard Choices: International Finance and Economic Adjustment in North Africa," in Dirk Vandewalle, *North Africa: Development and Reform in a Changing Global Economy* (New York: St. Martin's Press, 1996), pp. 25-63.

9. Reuters, "Morocco's 1994 Budget," news dispatch, Rabat, November 29, 1995. $1 equals approximately 9 Dirhams.

10. The World Bank, *World Development Report 1995* (New York: Oxford University Press, 1995); The World Bank, *World Development Report 1997*.

11. Interview with Fathallah Oualaâlou, Leader of the Socialist Union of Popular Forces Parliamentary Group, in Rabat, Morocco, August 14, 1993.

12. George Sabagh, "The Challenge of Population Growth in Morocco," *Middle East Report* 23:2, March-April 1993, p. 32.

III

The Monarchy, the *Makhzen* and the State

Moroccan society has experienced significant social and economic changes in the last 20 years. These changes have undermined the traditional social support that the monarchy has enjoyed in the past, partly destroying the system of notables that had provided the structures of political and social mobilization and control. This system was based on a rural elite submerged in traditional tribal structures, and included rural elected officials, religious nobility, and landowners. According to Remy Leveau, this elite allowed a central authority to use tribal structures to control the countryside.[1] The rural elite was seriously weakened by major demographic changes, new urban dynamics, and changes in the patterns of exploitation of material and human resources. The importance of the rural elite to the regime also declined as the state and its administrative apparatus gradually penetrated the countryside—driven mostly by security and stability concerns—and as new urban notables emerged.[2]

A rising educated, urban middle class became an increasingly important player in the social system, gradually replacing the rural support that the monarchy had relied upon. To avoid detachment from new and important societal forces, the state and the monarchy had to seek out new social relations. This became an urgent task: further disconnection between the state and these new social forces would have made consensus on managing change even more difficult than it already was.

This social mutation did not, however, translate into the rise of civil society, nor did it lead to strong and sustained challenge to existing state-society relations, as was the case in neighboring Algeria. The king adapted by seeking new bases of support through controlled economic and political liberalization, without, however, encouraging independent movements of popular mobilization or deconcentrating power.

While democratization and its constitutive elements have lacked much substance in Morocco, repeated references to them in most official and opposition discourse have made them almost a permanent feature of political discourse. In reality, however, Morocco lacks the democratic process that one would expect to find in a country where associative life pre-dates independence and where multipartism is a permanent fixture. This contradiction can be observed when examining the nature of that associative life from a perspective of power relations between state and society. To do so requires, first, an analysis of the nature of the state and regime in place.

The Monarch

Morocco is a constitutional monarchy in which power is theoretically shared by the king, the government, and the parliament. In reality, however, most power is concentrated in the hands of the monarch. The current constitution, adopted in 1992 and amended by referendum in 1996, formally gives executive powers to the government and the parliament. The 1996 reform added a Chambre des Conseillers (Chamber of Counselors) and altered the structures of representation and election. The significance of the 1996 constitutional reform is examined later in this book.

While parliament initiates legislation, the king must sign on before it becomes law; he can dissolve parliament by decree and call for new elections, and can propose his own legislation for popular approval by way of referendum. He can also declare a state of emergency, rule by decree, and sign and ratify international treaties. He appoints the prime minister and the cabinet, and presides over the meetings of the cabinet, as well as those of the Supreme Judicial Council whose members are appointed by royal decree. A High Court of Justice handles crimes and felonies committed by members of government during their tenure. Its members are elected by parliament, while its president is selected by the king.

Morocco has a multiparty system, but the overwhelming dominance of the monarch limits the ability of the various parties to directly affect policies. No party challenges the supremacy of the king, and, at one point or another, many parties have joined coalition governments formed under pro-monarchy formations. However, a substantial change took place in February 1998 when, for the first time ever, the king appointed a prime minister from the opposition party, the Socialist Union of Popular Forces (USFP), which had won most seats in the lower house of parliament following the November 14, 1997 elections. This change and its political significance are discussed later in this book.

King Hassan II was born on July 9, 1929 and came to power on March 3, 1961, after the death of his father, Mohammed V, who had ruled since 1927. Mohammed's father, Mulay Hassan I, ruled Morocco from 1873 to 1894. From 1894 to 1908, Morocco was ruled by Abd al-Aziz, the son of Hassan I. He was succeeded by Mulay Abd al-Hafidh who ruled until 1927.

Hassan II is the twenty-first ruler of Morocco from the Alawi dynasty, which claims to descend from the Prophet Mohammed and which has ruled Morocco since 1666. Lacking the charismatic appeal of his father, who was also considered a nationalist hero, Hassan II had to use other means to consolidate his power and avoid becoming a figurehead king in a constitutional monarchy. He put the army and the police under his direct control and neutralized his main political opposition, the Union Nationale des Forces Populaires (National Union of Popular Forces, known as UNFP), by a variety of tactics.

Today, King Hassan's authority is well established in Morocco and widely respected in the world. At home, his legitimacy has been based mostly on traditional sources. Because of his ancestry, he is considered *amir al-mu'minnin* (the commander of the faithful), that is, a religious leader of the Muslim community. As such, he commands high respect among the people.

Using religious, historical, and constitutional sources of legitimacy, the king affords himself all powers possible, even those not specifically granted by the constitution. As a commander of the faithful, he is above the secular norms of the constitution. This quality alone, however, has not been enough to govern a society fragmented into groups representing different interests and tendencies. The secular opposition and the skeptics are kept in line by those loyal to the king—the army's officer corps, the security services, the police—and by patronage, clientelism, and a selective distribution of privileges. In short, King Hassan maintains his throne by appealing to the masses as a symbol of religious leadership, and by checking and manipulating a potentially dangerous elite. It is important to note here that several "[a]nthropologists, like many other Western observers, have tended to exaggerate both the religious and political significance of Hassan II's sanctity while completely overlooking his use of force and fear."[3]

King Hassan II rules through a mix of concentration of powers, repression of the opposition, and parliamentary politics. When his political position improved slightly at the beginning of the Western Sahara campaign in the middle of the 1970s, he eased restrictions on political life—but only to the extent not detrimental to the throne. He released some political prisoners, lifted press censorship, allowed municipal and provincial elections, and finally, after several postponements, parliamentary elections in 1977 and 1993. By 1998, the bloc of parties loyal to him still maintained its control over parliament and the government. The parliamentary elections of November 14, 1997 did not really alter Morocco's political map and power distribution, in spite of the appointment of a member of the opposition as prime minister.

The *Makhzen*

The notion of *makhzen* appears in many studies of the Moroccan polity and state. The noun *makhzen* is derived from the Arab verb *khazana* which means to hide away, to store, or to preserve. At the time of the Arab-Muslim empire (during the extension of the Muslim Empire to Morocco, starting the 700s AD), the *makhzen* was the chest in which the *emirs* stored tax monies destined for the Khalif. Later on, the word referred to the treasury (*dar al-makhzen*). In contemporary Morocco, *makhzen* became synonymous with central power.[4] Today, the *makhzen* is an instrument of legitimation that uses religion, history, and authority to obtain the obedience of people; it controls territory through administrative authorities, adjudicates conflicts between groups, and defines symbols of national unity and identity.

According to Alain Claisse, the *makhzen* constitutes a patrimonial form of power, but unlike the monarchy, it can be publicly contested. As a centralized form of authority, it combines traditional and modern types of "leadership which aim at consolidating the social base of power...." The traditional form of leadership links the monarchy to various clients who obtain services, prestige, and goods in return for their support. The modern type of leadership seen in the *makhzen* is an institutional and normative power that provides "rules and authorizations of economic activities, nominations to prestigious or high paying offices, and mobilization of support through peasant and cultural organizations."[5] Traditional *makhzen* agents and modern state institutions (e.g., pashas, khalifas, caids, and governors) combine to form the Moroccan state on top of which the monarchy stands. Whenever *makhzen* instruments of authority seemed to fail, the king expanded the modern state administration, through the powerful Ministry of the Interior, which established tight control of people and territory. Jean-Claude Santucci observed that while management is left to the modern state and its technocrats, the *makhzen* governs people "through the control of power networks, matrimonial exchanges, and through actual arbitrations and the distribution of wealth."[6] Furthermore, and as Santucci has found, the *makhzen* does not allow for the organization of autonomous entities within its political territory because that would erode its control over politics and social reproduction. This institutional behavior inhibits one of the most important prerequisites of civil society—the development of independent associative entities capable of checking the power of the state (and in this case, the *makhzen*) and the ability to mobilize societal interests to affect public policy. Because of the logic of the *makhzen* state and the limitations it imposes on independent power centers, the Moroccan political community is more prone to seek closeness to the system rather than to challenge it and press for meaningful social, economic, and political changes.

In sum, to understand the relationship that exists between state and society in Morocco, it is not enough to look at the formal aspects of the modern state institutions and processes. Many important decisions are made in the elusive realm of the *makhzen*, which constitutes informal yet powerful behavioral institutions and power sources. Therefore, the modern concept of state alone provides an insufficient framework for understanding Moroccan state-society relations. Any discussion of civil society must thus take into account the particular social-political phenomena of the *makhzen*.

Challenges and Revolt

During his reign, the strongest challenges King Hassan II has faced have come from the army and the "street." In 1971 and 1972, the monarch was the target of failed coup attempts organized by the army. Another plot was discovered in 1983. After having escaped unharmed, the king further centralized military powers, and succeeded in rallying most political forces behind him over the irredentist claims on the Western Sahara. In the last 25 years, the king has diminished the potential for a coup through purges, executions, and imprisonments of military officers, and beginning in 1975 by dispatching most of the army to the Western Sahara, south of the internationally recognized border, in a campaign to annex that territory after Spain vacated it. This campaign started in the form of a popular "Green March" and was met with strong military resistance by a Sahrawi independence movement, which had the support of Algeria and Libya, and by UN resolutions calling for a referendum among the local population over the future status of the territory.

As the annexation of the Western Sahara settled into a long and costly war, and as economic conditions worsened for the majority of the population, popular discontent and unrest led to further restrictions on political life. Parliamentary elections were postponed several times and dissidents were jailed. Youth and economically disadvantaged segments of society also challenged King Hassan's leadership and policies with wide-scale riots in 1965, 1981, 1984, and 1990, and limited ones throughout the 1990s (e.g., the Tangier riots of June 1996).

In the early 1980s, the king moved to regain the confidence of the masses. In August 1984, he signed a treaty with Libya which promised, among other things, new job opportunities in Libya for young Moroccans. At that time Morocco had already opted for the structural adjustment program which was officially presented as necessary for economic growth and a better life for all Moroccans. In the wake of these moves, and as a result of popular mobilization behind the annexation of the Western Sahara, people regained some confidence in their monarchy. But this confidence remained fragile as economic conditions did not improve for most Moroccans.

Notes

1. Remy Leveau, *Le Fellah Marocain Défenseur du Trône* (Paris: Press de la Fondation Nationale des Sciences Politiques, 1976).

2. For a succinct analysis of the decline of the rural elite in Morocco, see Mohammed Brahimi, "Grandeur et Décadence des Elites Rurales," in Noureddine El-Aoufi, ed., *La*

Société Civile au Maroc (Rabat, Morocco: Societé Marocaine des Editeurs Réunis, 1992), pp. 171-183.

3. Henry Munson, Jr., *Religion and Power in Morocco* (New Haven, CT.: Yale University Press, 1993), p. 147.

4. Alain Claisse, "Le Makhzen Aujourd'hui," in Jean-Claude Santucci, ed., *Le Maroc Actuel: Une Modernisation au Miroir de la Tradition?* (Paris: CNRS, 1992), p. 285.

5. Ibid., p. 288. (Translation mine).

6. Jean-Claude Santucci, "Etat et Société au Maroc: Enjeux et Perspectives du Changement," in Jean-Claude Santucci, ed., *Le Maroc Actuel: Une Modernisation au Miroir de la Tradition?* (Paris: CNRS, 1992), p. 429. (Translation mine).

IV

International Opportunities and Constraints

Domestic political systems do not evolve in a vacuum. Over the last century, it has become difficult for political leaders to shield their societies from international influences. In the case of Morocco, international opportunities, pressures, and constraints have strongly affected domestic politics, particularly in the last 20 years. Any discussion of state-society relations in general, and of civil society in particular, is enhanced by a consideration of the interplay of international events and policies with domestic social, economic, and political dynamics. Morocco's internal developments have been affected by two major international factors: the Western Sahara conflict, and economic transformations in the world in general, and in Europe in particular.

The Western Sahara Conflict

The Western Sahara conflict, which began in 1975, required major military, economic, and political resources and affected Morocco in two ways. First, the campaign imposed a major financial burden on the state budget and accelerated the economic crisis of the early 1980s. Second, the campaign allowed the king to skillfully rally support for the monarchy and the state under the nationalist banner. He kept the opposition in line by labeling it anti-nationalist and repressing any dissent. Moreover, the military threat to the monarchy diminished after the army was mobilized for the Western Sahara annexation and also for an eventual armed conflict with Algeria, the main supporter of the Polisario liberation movement. Therefore, while the conflict carried a tremendous economic cost for Morocco, it also produced a major political payoff for the regime by neutralizing the opposition.

The International Economic Environment

As state resources were drawn down to pay for the Western Sahara campaign, and as foreign sources of capital diminished, it became difficult for Morocco to satisfy the basic needs of economic growth. Foreign capital became scarce throughout the Maghrib as new investment opportunities opened up in Eastern Europe in the late 1980s. The huge debt accumulated by the Third World led several lending institutions to limit their support to the developing world in general. Moreover, the European Community's move toward fuller economic integration following the 1992 Maastricht Accord threatened Morocco's relevance to the continent's economy.

In the international economic environment of the 1980s, which was marked by a general drop in economic performance, even developed countries went into recession; in the early 1990s, the European and US growth rates experienced a net decline. This in turn slowed international trade and led to further Western import restrictions. Morocco's exports suffered directly from this trend and its debt position worsened, even though it was by then engaged in the IMF-sponsored structural adjustment program. Moreover, a series of droughts in the mid-1980s devastated agricultural production and led to a sharp rise in food imports.

The combination of these international economic factors with the droughts, the financial burdens of the Western Sahara campaign, and debt servicing seriously limited Morocco's ability to weather the economic crisis and to face mounting social and political tensions. In addition to these economic constraints and with the end of the cold war, the West's promises of economic assistance (in the form of aid, debt rescheduling, and access to international capital) were made dependent on progress in economic and political liberalization and on respect for human rights. These conditions constituted added pressure on Morocco for political change in addition to that for economic restructuring.

The Impact of the Gulf War

The 1991 Gulf War and the rise of the Islamist challenge in the

Maghrib—mainly in Algeria and Tunisia—further strained the Moroccan political and economic system. By disturbing economic interaction between Arab states, the Gulf War sharply diminished financial assistance to, and investments in, Morocco from the Gulf states, mainly Saudi Arabia and Kuwait. In addition, because of the Gulf War and the perceived Islamist threat in the Maghrib, several Western governments and private businesses hesitated to commit funds and investments to the region. Tourism also suffered as fewer and fewer Westerners ventured into Arab countries in the aftermath of the Gulf War.

The Gulf War also widened the existing gap between Maghribi societies and their governments as people protested their leaders' formal "neutrality" in the conflict or indirect acquiescence to the US-led coalition against Iraq. Unable to contain popular support for Iraq, King Hassan—who had committed 2,000 troops to the defense of the Muslim holy places in Saudi Arabia—had to allow a general strike called by political parties and labor unions in support of the Iraqis, and a massive demonstration condemning the war and calling for the withdrawal of Moroccan troops from the allied coalition. As in Algeria and Tunisia, the Gulf War protests in Morocco provided a unique opportunity for Islamists to openly mobilize new sympathizers and to articulate popular demands. "In Morocco, the Gulf War gave the Islamists public exposure for the first time and without repression from the state. For the first time, [they] appeared as a legitimate force alongside the secular opposition parties."[1] But as the years to come would show, this was a rare exception to the limitations usually placed on Islamist activism in Morocco. Indeed, after the war, the Islamists' status in the political arena returned to what it was in 1990; it was not tolerated.

The international and regional economic and political events discussed above have had profound effects on the political evolution of Morocco over the last 20 years. These effects include:

❖ A weakening of the political opposition as a direct result of the national mobilization around the Western Sahara campaign.

❖ Further tightening, in the late 1970s and early 1980s, of the limitations imposed on the autonomy of social and political groupings, in the name of national unity in the face of regional challenges (i.e., the Western Sahara and Algeria). For example, civic associations and movements not connected to the traditional parties or promoted by the state had a hard time gaining recognition.

❖ The relative opening of the political system, in the form of municipal elections in 1992 and 1997 and parliamentary elections in 1993 and 1997; a slight increase in the freedom of the press by the mid-1990s; and an amnesty for political prisoners in 1994. These actions resulted from domestic pressures, but also—and perhaps primarily—from international pressures for political liberalization as a condition for economic assistance (debt rescheduling and IMF support for economic restructuring) and for a special relationship with the European Union.

❖ An escalation in the crackdown of the Moroccan Islamist opposition in response to increased activism in its ranks but also as an indirect result of the violent conflict in Algeria between radical Islamists and the regime since 1991.

These developments and their impact must be taken into consideration in any attempt to explain the recent internal evolution of Morocco. As summarized above, they prompted certain policies, provided civic groups with unique opportunities to attempt to impose their will in the political arena, and justified certain state policies which would not have been tolerated under other circumstances.

Notes

1. Azzedine Layachi and Abdel-Kader Haireche, "National Development and Political Protest: The Islamists in the Maghreb," *Arab Studies Quarterly* 15:2-3, Spring-Summer 1992, p. 89.

V

Civil Society and Associative Life

As indicated earlier, scholars and politicians have defined civil society in many ways, ranging from the very general to the most specific. However, there seems to be minimum agreement on thinking of civil society as the activities of a variety of actors for the purpose of participating—directly or indirectly—in the decisionmaking process through the independent aggregation and articulation of interests and opinions. These actors include associations, political parties, trade unions, the independent press, independent individual actors such as intellectuals, and various informal groupings of a cultural, religious, or other nature.

In any country where state-society interactions are characterized by the existence of a civil society, the key players are usually associations, parties, and unions. However, most studies on civil society tend to focus on civil associations and to underplay—or ignore—the role of political parties.[1] In the case of Morocco, scholars are even more inclined to dismiss the role played by political parties because most established parties are closely connected to the state and its traditional corollary, the *makhzen*. Moroccan parties are conservative in the face of a society yearning for change, and have lost much of their power to mobilize and articulate societal interests. However, in a search for indices of civil society, political parties should not be overlooked because they greatly affect associative life.

In the last 20 years, there has been a marked proliferation of Moroccan civic associations which have managed to take the lead in popular action when parties and unions failed to do so. This associative mobilization remains, however, constrained by the political environment of the day and by a watchful state. This phenomenon is examined in detail in the sections below.

A Perennial Associative Life

As in most societies, associative life and activities are not new in Morocco. They pre-date independence. Traditional types of associations were often informal and most of them evolved around collective efforts to deal with the normal difficulties of life at the community or village level. These include Djama'a, Touiza, Mouzara'a, and Mousakat, which are categories of informal associations that existed throughout the rural areas. These traditional associations usually had a fairly homogeneous membership since they were limited to the inhabitants of rural villages or towns. They were spontaneous and pragmatic associations that constituted forms of community self-help in areas such as agriculture, irrigation, food stocks, and even religious teaching.[2] But as Moroccan society evolved and small communities changed, this form of associative life began to disintegrate. New types of associations, mostly concentrated in urban centers, were born in the 1970s and 1980s. Whereas the traditional types of spontaneous and utilitarian associations were mostly rural and out of the reach of state control, the new urban ones drew the suspicion of the state and the monarch and aroused the interest of political parties and urban notables. These associations were approached—and even used—by political parties and individuals for electoral and personal advancement.

There are approximately 30,000 associations in Morocco today of varying sizes, activities, purposes, and memberships. Many of them are, however, highly influenced by the political and social environments in which they evolve, and this often contributes to their inefficiency as independent aggregators and articulators of grassroots demands. They often serve as top-down relays between the political sphere and society, and many of them are used by the state as instruments of ideological integration.

While freedom of association has been guaranteed and exercised since the Royal Charter of 1958 and the Dahir (Royal Decree) of November 27 of the same year, the inclusion of the citizenry in the management of the social, economic, and cultural affairs of the country has remained fairly limited to whatever the state has allowed from time to time. Both inclusion and exclusion also have been conditioned by the role of political parties as well as by the members' own beliefs about their participatory right or potential. In general terms, the inclusion trend (i.e., allowing associative life to develop into a functioning civil society) has been sporadic and more often than not altogether absent. Several factors have contributed to this, as we shall see.

Obstacles to Civil Society

Abdallah Saaf, professor at the Faculté de Droit of Mohamed V University, argues that several objective and subjective factors work against the birth and development of civil society in Morocco. These factors are structural; they include the institutions, dominant social ideas, and the political ideology and culture.[3] The configuration of political life and the political tendencies of various players contribute directly to inhibiting the development of a civil society. This situation led Saaf to conclude that in Morocco today "the structure of the political universe is incompatible with the emergence of civil society."[4]

Similar pessimism was expressed by Khalid Jamai, Editor-in-Chief of the Istiqlalian newspaper *L'Opinion*. Jamai believes that the obstacles to the emergence of a civil society are not only institutional, but also, and most importantly, in the minds of many Moroccans. He explained that popular culture discourages innovation and individual achievement, and underestimates a person's ability to change his or her condition. With this frame of mind, the efforts necessary for the birth and development of a civil society are not even attempted.[5]

The Istiqlal Party was founded in 1943 as a nationalist movement for independence and is formally committed to a tolerant Islam which it recognizes as an important source of Morocco's social, political, and cultural values. If post-independence Morocco had opted for a one-party system, the Istiqlal party would probably have been that party.

Moreover, and before concluding that "civil society in Morocco is an aberration," Jamai explained that Morocco is essentially a religious system in which the concept of citizen—which is central in the Western conception of democracy—does not exist. Abdallah Saaf adds elsewhere that the attitude of apoliticism of Moroccans may be due to the fact that the dominant perception of politics is that of a vast system of compromise, exchange, and mutual favors. For most Moroccans, politics seems like an instrument of advancement for those who practice it and not necessarily a collective endeavor for the realization of the national objectives unanimously agreed upon.[6]

There are many other obstacles to political liberalization and democratization and, thus, to the development of a civil society as defined here. They include the attitude of the political elite, the role of the *makhzen*, and legal and administrative limitations.

From interviews conducted with leaders of associations and of established parties, it appears that some members of the elite—party leaders—resist the idea of an autonomous mobilization of differentiated interests unless they have some influence over the associations representing these interests. This explains why new associations are more likely to be accepted if they are linked to an established political party.

In Morocco, the political elite constitutes "the spine" of the state with which it is identified. It perpetuates clientelist and neo-patrimonial relations with society and, thus, is not expected to provide a vanguard leadership for the establishment of a civil society.[7] On the contrary, its interests and position within the system could be threatened by civil society.

Moreover, as stated in Chapter III, the state-*makhzen* regards some areas and activities as too sensitive to be left to the discretion of autonomous associations. As a result of this attitude, the state often undertakes various actions and policies to inhibit the independent mobilization of differentiated interests around cleavages such as class, or regional or ethnic affiliation. These actions and policies have included the promotion of state-sponsored regional cultural associations and the denial of legal status to certain independent associations.

The state fears that an independent associative mobilization could lead to dynamic and autonomous processes that may weaken the control of society by hegemonic state institutions. The ultimate goal is to eliminate any potential opposition to regime, state, and king. The consequence of such policies has been a "makhzenization" of society, i.e., an almost total control of society by the state through various administrative, cultural, political, and police means. In the end, people find themselves in a "situation of social and economic dependence vis-à-vis the makhzenien state through a clientelist relationship."[8]

Not all associations in Morocco have been subjected to strict limitations. The watchful state has focused its control mostly on associations that actually—or potentially—challenge the state or its policies (human rights associations, radical Islamist associations, and labor unions). The clearest limitation imposed on the expression of a genuine civil society has come in the form of legal-administrative constraints.

This often indirect, yet powerful, type of limitation usually comes in the form of legal and administrative obstacles (red tape) instituted to prevent certain associations from acquiring a legal status. For the associations that have already acquired legal status, the state controls their activities by way of inhibitive legal requirements, such as complicated legal procedures for activity permits, or strong financial incentives that encourage only activities deemed appropriate. Article 9 of the Moroccan constitution guarantees "freedom of opinion, freedom of expression in all its forms and freedom to assemble." It also guarantees "freedom to organize and freedom to join any trade union or political organization."[9] However, any association that challenges national integrity or the monarchy is automatically prohibited by the Dahir of 1958. In 1973, amendments to this law limited further the right to associate (Dahir of April 10, 1973). The amended law obligates every association to apply for legal status by submitting a "Déclaration Préalable," a preliminary written statement on the nature and purposes of the association. Before 1973, any association could be created and become active without prior legal recognition. But since the 1973 amendment, no association can be formed without a Déclaration Préalable and formal state approval. Of course, administrative action on a request for legal recognition can be delayed indefinitely if someone in the power structure does not wish to see the applying association come into existence. Moreover, on the basis of this same amendment, the administrative authority can suspend or dissolve any association which fails to submit an application. In either case—suspension or dissolution—the executive officers of these associations can be held personally responsible and fined or sentenced to a maximum of two years in prison.

In 1988, a group of technocrats created a new party, the Parti Unioniste du Maghreb-Arabe (Unionist Party of the Arab-Maghreb, known as PUMA). Ten years later, in 1998, its application for official recognition has still not been approved. This party, which proposes to promote inter-Maghrib cooperation, was thus barred from all elections held since its creation. Its demand for recognition has not yet been answered by the Ministry of Interior and, therefore, as far as the state is concerned, the party does not officially exist.[10] As a consequence, it was not allowed to participate in the elections of 1997.

The 1973 amendment thus gave the state a powerful administrative tool with which to control associative life. Whether or not the state has chosen to use this tool against a particular association, however, has depended on the socio-political moment and on the nature and activities of the group. The decision rests on whether or not the proposed group is perceived as a potential threat to the state, the king, or the status quo.

It is important to note, however, that the state has not simply quashed all associative activities. In fact it has promoted many associations. For example, since 1983, the state explicitly encouraged the creation of regional cultural associations. These state-sponsored associations perform many functions, among them helping the state regulate and integrate the new social and political currents born in the wake of change. Also, the most active members of these associations have served as a leadership pool from which new state agents, notables, and even leaders for pro-monarchy parties have been recruited. Of course, these regional associations are not independent and therefore cannot be considered elements of civil society as defined above.

State restrictions have inhibited the development of an independent associative life, and set the limits of acceptable discourse. The restrictions, for example, forbid any questioning of Morocco's claim to the Western Sahara, prohibit attacks on Islam, and would harshly punish any criticism of the monarch, his decisions, or his leadership. Moreover, any associative action, regardless of its real intention, can be arbitrarily interpreted by state agents as a violation of these rules. The association or its leaders, or both, may face severe sanctions, as has often happened to human rights associations, radical Islamist associations, and Amazigh associations.

In spite of state interference with associative life, many associations have been fairly active and vibrant, albeit within the confines of restrictive laws and political dynamics. The relatively recent multiplication of urban-based associations was mostly stimulated by economic difficulties and by the subsequent state retreat from social services. As in Algeria in the early 1990s, the economic crisis in Morocco made the state unable or unwilling to assist many of the sectors of activity and social groups it had previously helped. In response to the crisis, as part of the structural adjustment program, Morocco attempted to restructure not only the economy but also its people's perception of the role of the state in the economy. The new perception underplays the role of state in the economy and promotes the idea of self-help.

During this period of economic, social, and institutional change, many sectors of society (fixed-income groups, unemployed youth, and rural populations) found themselves worse off as years passed and some of them rebelled against public policies or the absence of state services. The rebellion took the form of riots, strikes, and demonstrations and reflected the paradoxical combination of society's desire to be autonomous and people's expectation that the state remain a provider and a regulator. This contradictory attitude vis-à-vis the state encouraged the proliferation of associations but did not stimulate the structural changes necessary for the establishment of a civil society. In other words, hardship and receding institutional assistance stimulated the need for an associative life that would help alleviate that hardship. However, at the same time, Moroccans retained a high expectation for the state to provide services and to regulate the economy.

Notes

1. Political parties are included here because those in opposition perform some of the functions attributed to civil associations, such as challenging the power of state institutions and leaders, and questioning and attempting to influence public policies. Some authors include Islamist movements in their delimitation of civil society, while others exclude them because of their hegemonic ambitions. The Islamists are included here for the same reason political parties are.

2. Ahmed Ghazali, "Contribution à l'Analyse du Phénomène Associative au Maroc," in Michel Camau, ed., *Changements Politiques au Maghreb* (Paris: CNRS, 1991), pp. 243-261.

3. Abdallah Saaf, "L'Hypothèse de la Société Civile au Maroc," in Noureddine El-Aoufi, ed., *La Société Civile au Maroc* (Rabat, Morocco: Societé Marocaine des Editeurs Réunis, 1992), pp. 11-24.

4. Ibid., p. 13.

5. Khalid Jamai, Editor-in-Chief of *L'Opinion*, Interview with the author, Rabat, July 6, 1994.

6. Abdallah Saaf, "Tendances Actuelles de la Culture Politique des Elites Marocaine," in Jean-Claude Santucci, ed., *Le Maroc Actuel: Une Modernisation au Miroir de la Tradition?* (Paris: CNRS, 1992), p. 248. (Translation mine.)

7. Saaf, "L'Hypothèse," op. cit., p. 15.

8. Ibid., p. 16.

9. Constitution of Morocco, adopted by referendum in 1992 and amended in 1996.

10. Agence France Presse, "Un parti réclame sa reconnaissance par les pouvoirs publics," news dispatch, Rabat, April 7, 1997.

VI

Associations and the Independent Press

In Morocco, independent associations can be divided into three broad groupings based on the social classes and interests they represent. At the very top, there is a select group of private clubs and organizations of business owners; they include members of the political, cultural, and economic elite. At mid-level are political parties, unions, professional organizations, and various associations and groupings of the official press. Membership in these associations cuts across various social and economic groups. Abdallah Saaf, who previously denied the existence of civil society in Morocco, paradoxically refers to these two categories as the "official" civil society which is led and controlled by the intellectual and technocratic elite and the notables, expresses itself in writing, and is found in large cities. At the last level—the mass level—there are mystic sects, religious associations, the underground press, and ritual gatherings. Saaf calls this category the "silent" or "non-official" civil society which exists on the periphery, in the shantytowns of large cities and in the countryside, and expresses itself orally, with allusions and symbols only.[1]

Abdallah Saaf's categories of civil society are only heuristic insofar as they represent a given interpretation of a very complex reality, without necessarily explaining it. The notion of "silent" civil society contradicts, in fact, the most accepted definitions of civil society, because civil society is not supposed to be silent. A silent civil society is just non-existent.

To provide a tangible view of associative life in Morocco and its limitations, associations are presented here by area of activity. Most formal associations are located in the bigger cities of Morocco (Casablanca, Fez, Rabat, Marrakesh), and their membership is fairly young and educated. The urban middle class is well-represented in their ranks, and often uses them for collective action on given issues. Their activities cover a wide spectrum of interests: sports, the arts, religion, professional interests, humanitarian aid, human rights, etc. Associations representing the liberal professions (lawyers, doctors, architects, pharmacists) are among the most active, along with those representing the managers and owners of private enterprises, which are by far the most influential in the area of economic policy. The most recently created associations are those working on human rights, consumers rights, and environmental protection. Some associations have indirect links to political parties, such as the labor unions and associations of writers and economists that are known to have some sympathy for parties of the left and often serve as fora for party activities. Others associations try to maintain relative independence, even if they were originally created by militants of a party or group of parties (e.g., the Moroccan Organization of Human Rights, or OMDH). A last category, as mentioned earlier, includes associations promoted by the state to serve purposes of the state and the monarchy. Among the latter are regional cultural associations, which have multiplied in recent years, such as the associations of Angad el Maghreb Acharqui, Hawd-Assafi, Doukkala, Ahmed al-Hansali, Illigh, Annahda-Nador, and al-Mouhit.

Business Associations

Business associations are among the most active and effective associations because they are blessed not only with financial resources but also with a strong sense of purpose. Some of them represent a narrow business interest, while others coordinate between elements of the business sector in the areas of pricing, production, and trade practices. More importantly, and because of their power, they participate—often directly—in the state's economic decisionmaking. In fact, the large place occupied by private business in the Moroccan economic and political systems is mostly due to the power of these associations and their leaders.[2] The most important associations are those representing large corporations. Their leaders are often high administration officials as well as businessmen. The most important of these associations are:

❖ Confédération Générale Economique du Maroc (General Economic Confederation of Morocco, known as CGEM)
❖ Union Marocaine Agricole (the Moroccan Agricultural Union)

❖ Comité Professionnel de la Minoterie Marocaine (Professional Committee of Moroccan Mills)

❖ Fédération des Industries de Conserve du Maroc (Federation of Canning Industries of Morocco)

❖ Fédération Marocaine des Sociétés d'Assurance (Moroccan Federation of Insurance Companies)

❖ Fédération des Industries des Corps Gras (Federation of Industries of Fat Products)

❖ Association Professionnelle des Industries de Tannerie (Professional Association of Leather Industries)

❖ Association Marocaine de l'Industrie Textile (Moroccan Association of the Textile Industry)

❖ Association des Industries Minières (Association of Mining Industries)

❖ Association Professionnelle des Importateurs de Matériel (Professional Association of Materials Importers)

❖ Association Marocaine des Producteurs d'Agrumes (Moroccan Association of Citrus Fruit Producers)

These associations represent the core of Morocco's private business and wield an extraordinary power not only over economic policy, but also social legislation (i.e., minimum wage and workers' benefits). They coordinate their lobbying efforts and their influence through the CGEM and the Moroccan Agricultural Union. Their activities and actions are also coordinated through family and tribal networks, since many of their leaders are blood-related.[3]

The Labor Movement

Labor activism is not new in Morocco. Trade unionism originated and developed during the colonial period. The oldest labor organization is the Union Marocaine du Travail (Moroccan Labor Union, known as UMT). It was the sole labor union until 1960 when the Istiqlal party created a rival group, the Union Générale des Travailleurs Marocains (General Union of Moroccan Workers, known as UGTM). In 1963, the Movement Populair (Popular Movement) party created the Union Syndicale des Travailleurs Libres (Labor Union of Free Workers, or USTL), and in 1970, another union, linked to the Socialist Union of Popular Forces (USFP) party, was born: the Confédération Démocratique des Travailleurs (Democratic Labor Confederation, the CDT). The lat-

ter quickly overshadowed the UMT mostly because it was more combative. However, "[despite] the UMT's historical role and the CDT's
occasional success in opposing the regime, the political and economic
climate in Morocco remains hostile to the development of a vigorous
and independent labor movement."[4]

Other parties also created their own unions, thereby contributing
to the proliferation of groups that have mitigated against unified labor
action. These other unions include the National Union of Moroccan
Workers, the Federation of Popular Unions, the Moroccan Labor Forces,
the National Popular Union, the Association of Moroccan Workers and
the Moroccan Workers Union.

Unions of liberal professions are often linked to parties, since a
totally independent union has little chance of succeeding in Morocco.
In 1994, for example, unions of writers, journalists, engineers, economists, and lawyers were all headed by members of the USFP. However,
their membership includes elements or sympathizers of several parties.
In an interview, Fathallah Oulaâlou, leader of the USFP parliamentary
group and president of the Moroccan Writers' Union (Syndicat des
Ecrivains Marocains), explained his party's heavy presence in the associative arena in the following terms: "Because they were kept out of
power, political parties invaded the social field and created associations
in order to increase their strength."[5]

Labor union activism in Morocco reached its peak in the 1970s,
but since then has been increasingly subdued by the interplay of various factors, including state repression, harassment and manipulation,
major divisions within the movement over strategies and means, conflict with political leaders—mostly party leaders—and a high level of
unemployment. As a result, the Moroccan labor movement as a whole
has slowly lost much of its combativeness, and its role of articulator of
workers' grievances and interests has suffered greatly. A nationwide
strike of train workers organized in the spring of 1995 exhibited some
of the contradictions and problems from which the union movement
suffers today. Even though the strike was observed for 28 days, its
organizers (the UMT, CDT, and UTM) were not totally in control of
developments. The union leaders expected the strike to last only few
days, hoping that the king would give in to their demands. When they
faced an unyielding monarch and an uncompromising state bureaucracy, they feared wide-scale repression and tried to call off the strike.
However, the workers wanted to continue until some of their demands

were met. In the end some were, but the unions and the parties they were affiliated with (mainly the USFP) were left weakened by this show-down. The events showed the leadership's inability to control the mass of workers and exhibited its fear that mobilization of the rank and file could lead to either a "hijacking" by the Islamists or to state repression that would further weaken their organizations. Faced with this dilemma and with the harsh reality of their waning appeal, unions now appear more accommodating than combative.

Religious Associations and the Islamist Movement

Religious associations have always been numerous in Morocco. In general, they seek to help people adjust to the forceful pace of modernization without losing their Islamic faith and practice. They are of two general types: traditional and conservative associations, and modern and change-seeking associations. In the second category one finds several urban-based groupings which started in the 1970s to challenge the existing order and even the monarch himself.

In 1974, Abdesslam Yacine, a school teacher, challenged King Hassan II on religious and historical grounds. He sent him an open letter admonishing him to accept a six-point program for the "religious political redemption and salvation" of the king and the community. In that letter, Yacine questioned the legitimacy of King Hassan II and suggested that the monarch redeem himself by doing away with injustice, by committing himself to the renovation of Islam, and by making himself accountable to a council elected according to Islamic principles.[6] This open challenge to the king led to Yacine's internment for many years in a psychiatric hospital and jail. He is currently under house arrest.

When economic conditions worsened in the late 1970s and early 1980s, Islamist activism openly challenged not only King Hassan's policies and style of government, but also his claim to religious and traditional leadership. However, very early on, the monarch tried to head off such challenge by arresting many members of the radical Jam'iyat al-Shabiba al-Islamiyya (Islamic Youth, created by Abdelkrim Moutii and Kamel Ibrahim in 1970) and the Harakat al-Mujahidin (the Mujahidin Movement led by Abdessalam Naâmani). They were accused of plotting to overthrow the throne and to establish an Islamic state; a number of them were sentenced to jail terms and others to death. Some Islamist groups such as Yacine's al-'Adl wa al-Ihsan (Justice and Benevolence) and al-Jama'a al-Islamiyya (the Islamic Group) still enjoy wider popular support than the secular clandestine opposition groups of the left.

The king's legitimacy, which these groups question, has been based not on a distributive function of the state as in Algeria, but rather on traditional allegiance to the Alawite throne. King Hassan is the only Maghribi leader whose authority is based on religious grounds. He has cultivated both religious and traditional support, by reinforcing traditional religious structures and by balancing modernist actions with Islamic measures. These include the enactment of a Code of Personal Status (*Mudawana*) based on the Qur'an, the imposition of mandatory prayer in schools, the creation of Qur'anic schools and the establishment of a High Council of Ulamas to sanction his policies. In fact, the king established a whole system of expression of "official Islam," thereby monopolizing the religious sphere. In order to weaken any potential unified Islamist movement, he repressed the groups that could not be controlled (arresting 700 Islamists in 1982 alone and others in subsequent years), promoted the creation of several non-political religious organizations, and in 1980 reactivated the dormant Council of Ulama (religious scholars) and placed it under the control of the High Council of Ulama over which he himself presides. Paradoxically, this invigorated religious life, albeit stimulated and controlled by "official Islam," provided the Islamist movement with a favorable milieu for growth as a moral force.

Associations for *Da'wa* (preaching) multiplied with the encouragement of the state which also used them against its enemy—the secular left.[7] For example, Jama'at al-Tabligh wa al-Da'wa, a reformist monarchist group, found the situation particularly favorable to its growth. Created in 1965, the preaching association al-Tabligh Oual-Da'wa Lillah seeks the revival of the Islamic *umma* (Muslim community or nation) and the implementation of the Shari'a (Islamic law), but through peaceful means. It has several thousand members among urban dwellers. Most of these Da'wa associations are quite different from radical Islamist groups. Radical Islamist associations tend to appeal not to rural masses—traditional pillars of support for the monarchy—but to urban youth and disaffected segments of society. Radical groups tend to respond favorably to calls for the resurgence of religion, egalitarianism, and social solidarity.

By the early 1980s, there were some 23 religious associations, more or less politicized; some of them were part of international Islamist movements, while others were exclusively local. The Jam'iyat al-Shabiba al-Islamiyya, on the other hand, is a radical association created by Abdelkrim Moutii in 1970.[8] It rejects the existing order and seeks radical change. It has, however, lost most of its core and structure since the mid-1980s due to repression, factionalism, and divergent visions on how to combat the existing system. Its rival association is Yacine's al-'Adl wa al-Ihsan (Justice and Benevolence). Officially banned by the state in 1989, it has nonetheless increased its influence in recent years among the youth and the disaffected. Al-Jama'a al-Islamiyya was established in 1981 by former members of the Islamic Youth. Al-Rabita (the League) is a non-political benevolent religious association involved exclusively in social and humanitarian work. However, its principal task is to protect the interests and strengthen the brotherly relations of the *Shurafa* and their descendants.[9]

In Morocco, the Islamists have contended over the last 30 years with two monopolies over society: the control by the king of the religious arena, and the relative domination of the sphere of social and economic contestation by the traditional left—the unions and the leftist parties. The Islamists thus find themselves competing against well-established forces for the hearts and minds of the disaffected sectors of society and for the articulation of their wants and grievances. The only chance for the Islamists to acquire a voice in Morocco's politics would be an aggravation of the dislocations caused by the IMF austerity programs and the social and economic disengagement of the state, combined with a continued failure of the left to address and to articulate the grievances that arise from such dislocations. Although King Hassan has been able to co-opt, coerce, and contain the most visible manifestations of Islamism, the potential for an escalation of militant Islam remains a possibility, even if remote for now.[10]

Since the mid-1990s, the Islamists have increased their presence and activism in universities and high schools, notably by aggregating and articulating the various grievances that the students hold against their conditions and against public policy—or the lack of it. One of the most active groups is Yacine's al-'Adl wa al-Ihsan. This preaching association officially rejects the use of violence and does not attack the regime directly. In recent years it has targeted leftist parties and militants, some of whom were even physically attacked. This association is now seeking the right to form a political party that abides by the constitution and competes legally for power. Yacine's movement identifies itself with its Algerian counterparts Harakat Mujtama'a al-Silm (Movement of the Peace Society, known before April 1997 as Hamas, or Harakat al-Mujtama'a al-Islami, the Movement of the Islamic Society)[11] and Harakat al-Nahda (Renaissance Movement)—which are perceived as moderate Islamist parties—rather than with the radical al-Jama'at al-Islamiyya al-Moussalaha (Armed Islamic Group, known in Algeria as GIA) which uses violence as means to gain power and is responsible for the deaths of thousands of police and military personnel, as well as innocent civilians.

It is worth noting that except for Jam'iyyat al-Shabiba al-Islamiyya, which is almost non-existent today, most of the Islamist associations born in the 1970s "have evolved toward an 'Islamism of compromise' with the regime. Most known leaders have chosen the strategy of 'pressure' for the moralization of the political and socio-cultural life."[12] Many radical organizations were subdued by repression and weakened by internal division and by the inability to mobilize people for an upheaval against the regime. There exist, however, a few ultra-radical Islamist groups—some of which are suspected of having affinities with the Algerian GIA—which seem to be waiting for an opportune time to undertake violent action against the Moroccan regime.

The movement of Abdesslam Yacine, which claims to use moderate and legal means, benefited from the implosion of the other Islamist factions: it recruited their former members and attracted the sympathy of many young and disaffected urban dwellers. Al-'Adl wa al-Ihsan militants denounce social injustice and ethical degradation in Morocco and call for the return, through legal means, to the "rule of God," i.e., the implementation of the Shari'a.

In recent years, they have been able to penetrate various sectors of society, especially the poor neighborhoods and the schools and universities of Casablanca, Fes, Meknès, Marrakesh, and Rabat, and have recruited members even among educated urban professionals. As in Egypt, Algeria, and Tunisia, these Moroccan Islamists have garnered support through social and charitable activities in poor neighborhoods, by taking up the grievances of students against educational conditions and policies, and by attacking the corrupt political elite and its policies. Parallel to these actions, they have also undertaken a conscious effort to infiltrate political parties, labor unions, and civic associations for the sake of using them as a legal outlet for their criticisms and demands. This infiltration has reached a point where, according to Abderrahim Lamchichi, "Islamism seems now to touch all social strata of Morocco."[13]

In the parliamentary elections of November 1997, members of al-Tawhid wa al-Islah movement (Unity and Reform, led by Abdelilah Benkirane) ran as candidates of the Popular Democratic and Constitutional Movement (MPDC), a party of Islamist leaning, and won five seats. The MPDC has four of its members in the new parliament.

The Islamists in Morocco pose no imminent threat to the stability of the system at present. However, this may change, especially if a crisis were to arise over the transition of power (when King Hassan dies and/or leaves power to his son, Sidi Mohamed), or if the Islamists were to succeed in their efforts to move from the margins to the center of the political process through organized political action.[14] Some bold political actions undertaken recently by youth groups dominated by Islamist militants indicate a growing resolve of the movement's leadership to move to the center of the political process sooner rather than later. In the fall and winter of 1996-97, they organized sit-ins in several universities, demanded educational reforms in the name of all students, and called for the right to create a political party. Their resolve has been encouraged by several factors, including recent political reforms (parliamentary and electoral), the continued decline in popular support for established political parties, the worsening socioeconomic situation for most Moroccans, the impending transfer of power to Prince Sidi Mohamed, the conflict in Algeria, and relative gains in the protection of human rights thanks to pressures from domestic and international organizations.

Human Rights Associations

Human rights associations are relatively new in Morocco and have benefitted from international pressures on King Hassan to cease the persecution of political dissidents. In 1988, the Ligue Marocaine des Droits de l'Homme (Moroccan League of Human Rights) was created by a group of members of various opposition parties. This association is close to the Istiqlal party and is headed by Mohamed Ben Abdelhadi Kabbab. Another important organization is the Organisation Marocaine des Droits de l'Homme (Moroccan Organization for Human Rights) which is headed by Abdelaziz Bennani. These two organizations encounter various difficulties including state supervision, indirect threats against their leaders, and attempts by political parties and members of the elite to influence their actions. A third group, the Moroccan Human Rights

Association, headed by Abderrahmane Benameur, is subject to similar pressures and harassment. Two associations of lawyers have also been explicitly involved in the defense of human rights: the Moroccan Bar Association, headed by Abderrahim Jamai, and the Committee for the Defense of Human Rights, headed by Ahmed Abadrine. Overseas, Moroccan exiles in France created the Association pour la Defense des Droits de l'Homme au Maroc (Association for the Defense of Human Rights in Morocco), which publicizes human rights abuses in Morocco and pressures foreign governments and international organizations to look into these abuses.

To counterbalance the claims made by these independent associations and to respond to strong international pressures to improve its handling of human rights in Morocco, the state created an official 37-member Consultative Council on Human Rights headed by Secretary-General Mohamed Mikou. This council, which was appointed by King Hassan himself, set up groups to study prison conditions, revisions of the penal code, relations with foreign human rights groups, and the problem of people who are allegedly being held against their will by the Sahrawi Polisario in camps in the Tindouf area of Algeria. The council makes recommendations to the king for improvements in all these areas.

On November 11, 1993, a Ministry for Human Rights was created and Omar Azziman was appointed its minister; he was replaced in April 1995 by Mohamed Ziane. Furthermore, King Hassan slowly responded to international criticism of Morocco's human rights record—mostly from Amnesty International—by allowing the adoption of a national Charter of Human Rights in December 1990, freeing several hundred political prisoners between 1991 and 1993, and pardoning 4,957 common criminals in 1993. And, in July 1994, he answered long-standing complaints from Moroccan human rights groups by extending an amnesty to 424 more political prisoners. This amnesty applied even to Moroccans who had gone into exile for political reasons. In April 1994, the king approved the opening of a regional North Africa office of Amnesty International in Morocco. Of course, this office will not be permitted to monitor human rights in the host country.

In spite of these concessions, independent human rights associations in Morocco claim that neither the Moroccan state nor Amnesty International has addressed the cases of nearly 100 opposition figures who have "disappeared," and of those not defined by Moroccan authorities as political prisoners. The same is said about the more than

500 Sahrawis still reported as missing by Amnesty International and the Polisario.

It is clear, however, that the human rights situation in Morocco has improved since the early 1990s as a result of the combined pressure of domestic and international organizations and foreign governments. Much remains to be done in this area which is crucial to any democratization process, since people cannot be expected to participate freely and candidly in the political process if they are not guaranteed security and protection from persecution because of their ideas and beliefs.

Amazigh Associations

To some people, Morocco's Berber "minority" amounts to 40 percent of the population, while for others it is a majority of 65 percent. A third point of view is that Morocco, just like the rest of the Maghrib, is mostly Berber (in numbers and cultural identity) and that post-colonial regimes have pursued an ideology that denied this reality and promoted Arab culture and links to the Arab Mashriq. Most Amazigh associations that have developed around the issues of identity, culture, and language, have tended to accept the general "Arabist" ideology of Morocco and have limited their demands to an official acknowledgment of the existence of an important number of Moroccans who do not speak Arabic. They wish to promote the Tamazight language and culture in public arenas, such as schools and the media. There are, however, some Amazigh activists who wish to see the government give a larger place to the Amazigh component of Morocco's cultural identity.

Several Amazigh-based organizations promote the Tamazight language and Amazigh culture in Morocco. They include the Association Tellili (which means Freedom), the Association Marocaine de la Recherche et d'Echange Culturel (Moroccan Association for Research and Cultural Exchange, known as AMREC), and the less active association Assala, which promotes Moroccan cultural heritage. Three others should be mentioned even though they remain weak: Association du Bassin Méditerranée (Association of the Mediterranean Basin), Association Bine al Ouidane (Association of Bine al Ouidane), and Association Culturelle de Soussa (Cultural Association of Soussa).

On August 5, 1991, six associations (joined later by five others) met and signed what is called the Agadir Charter on the Amazigh culture and language in Morocco. In that text, these associations denounced "the systematic marginalization of Amazigh language and culture" and agreed to pursue seven goals, among them "the inclusion in the constitution of the national aspect of the Amazigh language next to Arabic," the "integration of the Amazigh language and cultures in various areas of cultural and educational activities, as well as in teaching programs," and the "right to coverage in the written, audio and visual mass media."[15]

In the wake of domestic and international calls for democratization, and also probably encouraged by popular Amazigh movements in Algeria in recent years, Moroccan Amazigh associations and leaders did not hesitate to take their demands to the street and ask for a state commitment to giving the Amazigh culture its rightful place in the national identity. During the 1994 Labor Day celebration, various pro-Amazigh banners were raised and many Amazigh slogans were chanted. Even though these public challenges to the status quo were repressed by the police,[16] political officials, including the king, later agreed to make some concessions. On June 14, 1994, Prime Minister Abdellatif Filali announced that national television would begin broadcasting a short version of the nightly newscast in Tamazight, and in an August 20 speech King Hassan spoke of "three Berber dialects" as being part of the national identity, and declared that "it was necessary, in the first grade at least, to reserve some hours for the teaching of our dialects." The king reaffirmed, however, that Arabic remained "the mother tongue" for all Moroccans.[17] Shortly after that speech, national television started broadcasting news in three Amazigh dialects (the state radio had been broadcasting programs in Berber for decades). For some Berber militants, this three-dialect TV news broadcast constituted an attempt to divide the Amazigh population by differentiating between three regional dialects rather than promoting a single Amazigh language. For others, it was a step in the right direction and a major state concession made because of associative activism.

Women's Associations

Women's associations developed mostly in the 1980s, though some date back to the 1960s. As a whole, these associations have been relatively successful in their work to promote and to protect Moroccan women in a rapidly changing environment. However, their actions have been limited by divisions among the leadership over the nature of actions to undertake—political action to defend women's rights in a patriarchal society or strictly humanitarian and cultural actions—by state control through financial incentives or administrative limitations, and by domination by political parties.

Official accounts indicate the existence of 29 voluntary women's associations, but non-official sources point to a much larger number of all kinds and in many areas. In the last decade alone, 10 such associations were created; some in the wake of a political overture by the king but most as a result of major social and economic changes which adversely affected the status and the lifestyle of women. In 1990, women's share in the urban labor force was 26.9 percent, while in 1960 it was only 12.9 percent. However, urban employment of women remains mainly in lower-status and lower-paid jobs.[18]

The state encouraged the activities of women's associations as instruments of popular mobilization around state programs and objectives. The state also needed them to help it deal with various social problems which it either could not handle alone or could not contain. There are today many women's associations—mostly in urban areas—that work on various social and cultural issues which the state no longer handles or was never interested in, such as the problem of unwed mothers, job training, and literacy for women. There are 19 women's associations in Rabat-Salé, five in Casablanca, two in Marrakesh, one in Meknès, one in Oujda, and one in the Western Sahara town of Lâayoune. These associations "provide services to materially and culturally deprived female strata, help raise the consciousness of women about their rights and duties, and contribute to their professional development and their integration in the low income professional sector."[19]

The Ministry of Youth and Sports and that of Craftwork and Social Affairs have special sections for women's affairs that organize various activities. They also provide funds for activities initiated by independent associations. The Ministry of Youth and Sport has even created 354 *foyers* (women's aid centers which provide some basic services) around the country, 180 of which are in rural areas. The need for such centers points to the increasing number of women who "fall through the cracks" and end up, for various reasons, without resources and shelter.

Often, the two avenues for women's activities—the official and the associative—clash. The independent associations try to articulate demands and initiate independent action, while the state bureaucracy tries to regulate, channel, and integrate women's activities into state programs that usually fall short of responding to the most basic needs of women and their condition. Independent associations which attempt to meet basic needs often lack sufficient human and material resources, and their actions are often hampered by diverging visions among the leadership on what women should and should not be doing for other women.

Some women believe their activities should be comprehensive and work toward establishing a movement capable of mobilizing women and defending their rights in a society dominated by men and regulated by patriarchal rules. Others believe women's actions should be limited to fulfilling fundamental human needs such as food, health, shelter, and basic education.

In an article on women's movements in Morocco, Moroccan sociologist Aicha Belarbi elaborated a typology of women's associations which distinguishes between humanitarian associations, family protection associations, and feminist associations.[20] Humanitarian associations include the Croissant Rouge (Red Crescent) and the Association de Soutient à l'UNICEF (Association of Support to UNICEF). While the first one includes activities that help women, the second promotes the objectives and programs of the international organization pertaining to children's problems and issues in Morocco.

There are six major family protection associations, among them the Association Marocaine de Planning Familial (Moroccan Association of Family Planning), the Association pour la Sauvegarde de la Famille (Association for the Safeguard of the Family), and the Association pour le Conseil des Familles (Association for Family Counseling).

Feminist associations comprise a variety of organizations that are active in the social, professional, and political arenas. The feminist groups focus on developing and strengthening women's awareness of their rights and obligations as mothers and citizens in the workplace and in the family. Many of the demands of the feminist associations are embedded in calls for reform of the *mudawana* (Code of Personal Status) which is perceived as a major obstacle to emancipation because it gives unequal rights and duties to men and women. Based in part on religious laws, it affords men many prerogatives over women.

Feminist organizations include social and professional associations, cooperative associations, and political associations. Social associations provide assistance to women in various areas, such as literacy, manual skills, housework, and bearing and raising children. The Union Nationale des Femmes Marocaines (National Union of Moroccan Women) is the most active association in this area. It was created in

May 1969 and was given the status of "association of public interests," which gives it access to state aid.

Professional associations promote women's emancipation and development in the workplace. They encourage women to study and develop careers, and help them mobilize for the defense of their own interests. Their actions are geared toward women in both the public and private sectors. They include: the Fédération des Femmes de Carrières Libérales et Commerciales (Federation of Women in Liberal and Commercial Careers), the Ligue National des Femmes Fonctionnaires dans le Secteur Public et le Secteur Privé (National League of Women Functionaries in the Public and Private Sectors), the Association des Femmes de Carrière Juridique (Association of Women in Legal Careers), and the Amicale Nationale des Cadres Féminins des Administrations Publiques et Semi-Publiques (National Association of Female Cadres of Public and Semi-Public Administrations).

Among feminist associations, the most active and most visible groups are those dealing with social and educational activities. Because their endeavors focus mostly on housework and raising children, they have been criticized for contributing to maintaining women in "minority" status. Also, since they interact closely with state institutions dealing with women and children, they are often perceived as status quo-oriented rather than as promoters of change. Professional associations remain limited in actions, membership, and scope. The number of professional women in the Moroccan workforce remains small, and their associations face the structural and political difficulties facing any independent mobilization attempts in the country. They must compete with the established labor unions, whose actions have a different focus.

Cooperative associations are pragmatic groupings that develop networks of mutual help between women and knit solidarity ties among them. They focus on providing women new manual skills and on income-earning activities, but also teach women how to work with others to promote the interests of all members of the group. These associations target housewives, young unemployed women, and skilled working women.

Several political associations include several women's groups, but none of them is totally independent from the parties. Many of these associations sprung from women's sections created within political parties, and they remain ideologically, and often structurally, linked to their respective parties of origin. Their actions are mostly limited to attracting women to the party and to mobilizing their support for the party's political agenda—especially during elections. However, three of these partisan "feminine sections" have transformed themselves into semi-independent associations of women. They do not answer to their party of origin, but remain committed to its ideological line. From the Party du Progrès et du Socialisme (Party of Progress and Socialism) came the Association Démocratique des Femmes Marocaines (Democratic Association of Moroccan Women), from the Organisation de l'Action Démocratique et Populaire (Organization of Democratic and Popular Action) came the Union de l'Action Féminine (Union of Feminine Action), and, finally, the Organisation de la Femme Istiqlalienne (Organization of the Istiqlalian Woman) came out of the Istiqlal Party.

Although they often undertake actions that are independent from political parties, these associations remain, in essence, partisan organizations: their ideological affinities lie with their parties of origin and their leadership always includes women party officers. These same officers are automatically members of the National Coordination Committee which serves as a formal link between the women's sections of all political parties. The Committee thus constitutes a *de facto* structural link between the associations and the parties.

Women's associations in Morocco are striving for greater participation in decision making regarding women's conditions in particular, and developmental programs in general. Their leaders seem to be fully aware of their potential impact; but they are equally cognizant of the great obstacles which they face in their professional, humanitarian, and political activities. However, as the state retreats further from the many social services it used to provide or control, women's associations are likely to increase in number, scope, and visibility. Also, whenever the political system opens up to more participation from organized social groups, women's associations may be poised to take advantage of this development. Their success will of course depend to a large extent on the ability of the leadership to resolve internal divisions and to lead the women's movement on a course that is relatively free from the party control which has plagued it since its inception.

The 1993 parliamentary elections produced, for the first time, two women deputies. Latifa Bennani Smires and Badia' S'qalli, from the Istiqlal and from the USFP respectively, were elected from a pool of 33 women candidates. This unprecedented event is certainly encouraging for Moroccan women, but much remains to be done to make women's social and political action an effective expression of civil society. To avoid the danger that this electoral gain will simply be a co-optation of women leaders, women's independent associative life must be strengthened and consolidated. In the long run, this may make women's social and political action an effective expression of a genuine Moroccan civil society. Many women activists believe that a movement toward that end must necessarily start with a major overhaul—if not the abolition—of the current Code of Personal Status, the *Mudawana*.

Youth and Student Associations

There are a number of youth and student associations, and their activities have, over the years, taken various forms and covered a wide range of interests, including sports, culture, career development, neighborhood concerns, and voluntary work. In general, however, these associations remain relatively weak and many of them are affiliated either with political parties (e.g., la Jeunesse du PPS—the PPS Youth) or with the government. Among the few active ones are the Fédération Marocaine des Associations de Chantiers (Moroccan Federation of Associations of Work Camps), which includes groups that do volunteer work in literacy, school construction, and even family planning; and Association des Chomeurs Diplomés (Association of Unemployed Graduates), which has been actively pushing for public policies that address the critical problem of unemployment among young graduates.

At the university level, the Union Nationale des Etudiants Marocains (National Union of Moroccan Students, UNEM) has recently come back to life after the state dissolved it in the 1970s to counter the influence of the left among youth. It was created by Mehdi Ben Barka when he was in the Istiqlal party. After an Istiqlal party splinter group created the UNFP, the UNEM became close to the latter (at least until the early 1970s). The Istiqlal party created its own student organization, the Union Générale des Etudiants Marocains (General Union of Moroccan Students, or UGEM) which has never had a strong appeal among university students.[21] Today, the UNEM, which is the most active student organization, seems to be controlled by the Islamist tendency, just like the leftist opposition controlled it in the 1960s and 1970s. Besides the highly politicized UNEM, students have no other legal and independent organization to express their practical interests and their political views.

The most dominant political tendencies within the university have been the left and the Islamists. On many occasions, violent clashes have taken place between them. In recent years, the Islamists have tried to lead student activism by mobilizing them around issues of common concern, such as university student transportation, and also for the recognition of an Islamist party.

The state has also been active in youth mobilization as a means both to integrate youth in national social and economic efforts and to neutralize radical activists. Besides keeping a close eye on independent student movements and organizations and repressing their most radical elements, the state created in 1990 the Conseil National de la Jeunesse et de l'Avenir (National Council of Youth and the Future), a consultative body on youth issues. This Council, which has accomplished very little, has mostly served as a means of moderating the debate on youth problems, such as unemployment and education, and has also been a tool for the co-optation of independent-minded and critical elements in society.[22]

Environmental Associations

There are of two types of environmental associations in Morocco: associations for the general purpose of protecting nature and safeguarding the environment, and environment-oriented associations with limited objectives. Associations of the first type plant trees, organize educational activities among the general public, and participate in scientific meetings relevant to the environment. Some of them are national, such as the Association Marocaine pour la Protection de l'Environnement (Moroccan Association for the Protection of the Environment) which was created in 1986, and the Mouvement National des Ecologistes Marocains (National Movement of Moroccan Ecologists). There are also many regional and local environmental associations which perform similar tasks.

Associations of the second category work on a specific scientific or professional project, and include the Société Marocaine pour le Droit de l'Environnement (Moroccan Society for Environmental Law), which was created in 1986; the Association Nationale pour la Production, Protection et Amélioration Végétale (National Association for the Production, Protection and Improvement of Plants), the Association Nationale pour la Production Animale (Association for Animal Production, ANPA), the Association Nationale des Améliorations Foncières, de l'Irrigation et du Drainage (National Association for Land Improvement, Irrigation and Drainage), and the Association Marocaine pour la Promotion des Energies Renouvelables (Moroccan Association for the Promotion of Renewable Energies) which was created in 1987.

There are many other associations that do not work directly on the protection of the environment, but whose activities reflect a concern for it. They range from associations working for the protection of old cities and landmarks to those interested in the protection of animals such as dogs and birds. They are too numerous to list here. Most environmental associations are either dormant or at an infant stage. They are constrained by the lack of public interest in environmental issues and thus by low membership. They are very small and lack financial and material means, as well as national and regional coordination.

Health Associations

There are many health-related associations in Morocco that are relatively active in their efforts to support and counsel people afflicted with certain disorders or diseases and their families. The Association Marocaine pour la Lutte Contre le SIDA (Moroccan Association for the Fight Against AIDS, or ALCS) is among the most active ones. Since 1988, ALCS has presented itself as a truly independent organization that works for the prevention of infection and cares for people who are infected with the HIV virus or have developed AIDS. At a Maghribi workshop on the role of non-governmental organizations (NGOs) in sustained development, organized in July 1993 in Rabat, two members of ALCS, Hakima Himmich and Latifa Imane, made a powerful statement on the notion of civil society and the limitations it faces in the Moroccan context. In one of their many writings on the subject, they assert that civil society "remains tightly linked to, if not prisoner of, the political environment, be it of the left or the right. This 'politicized' conception often, if not always, places civil society in the universe of unions, political parties, etc..."[23] Rejecting such a conception, Himmich and Imane called attention to a new associative phenomenon that they termed "multidisciplinary associations" or "associations with multiple identities." These associations work together as partners to complement each other and to share resources. This new type of civil association is located at the margin of the political world; it brings together people of different beliefs, reflects the reality of individuals and communities, and is far removed from electoral or strictly political ambitions and interests. ALCS represents this "new type of civil society." ALCS was created by medical doctors who faced two difficulties: the disease itself and the inability to speak openly about it in the public arena. The goal of these doctors became that of creating an arena of solidarity and prevention apart from any ideological, partisan, or governmental conception. "Our autonomy is the basis of our strength and our credibility among the different groups of people that we serve."[24]

International Non-Governmental Organizations

Morocco also has had a long tradition of involvement of international non-governmental organizations (INGOs) which have helped fulfill basic human needs and have provided disaster relief. Therefore, in addition to home-grown associations, a long list of international non-governmental organizations operates in Morocco. Many of them are benevolent Catholic entities and have been helpful in two ways. First, they have assisted many people in need through various charitable projects and educational programs. Second, they have helped develop a sense of modern associative life and action among many people in various parts of Morocco, mostly in rural areas.

Catholic Relief Services (CRS), an international organization created in 1917, operates in many countries around the globe. It provides disaster relief, helps in social and economic development, and organizes food programs. Most of its funds come from charitable contributions collected in US Catholic churches. It became operational in Morocco right after independence in 1956. Since then, CRS has helped the poorest Moroccans through food programs, educational projects, and community development programs. CRS has recently expanded its programs and increased its cooperation with governmental agencies working on similar projects.

Save the Children is an international organization of British origin that has been active in Morocco since 1960. It has concentrated its efforts on educating poor children and providing them with adequate food, clothing, and health care, and has paid a particular attention to handicapped children.

Terre des Hommes is a Swiss organization that was created in 1960 to help unwed mothers and their children, as well as handicapped individuals. Its centers are places where unwed mothers can go for the assistance they are unable to get elsewhere for social and cultural reasons. Terre des Hommes helps these women reintegrate into society, find jobs, and overcome administrative difficulties. It also cares for abandoned children and the children of unwed mothers. The group also helps children of various social origins who have health problems that the parents are unable to handle or that cannot be treated in Morocco—several children have been treated overseas, all expenses paid.

Comité d'Entraide International (CEI) was created by the French Evangelic church in 1969 and focuses mainly on fighting poverty. It has helped various communities establish self-help cooperatives in agriculture, health, education, and vocational training. Its activities are supported not only by the local Evangelical church but also by some American and German churches. CEI helped create an environmental association called Association de la Lutte Contre l'Erosion et la Desertification (Association for the Fight Against Erosion and Desertification).

While the contribution of INGOs is generally welcomed by most people who benefit from it and by government officials who find it helpful, some Moroccans have a less positive attitude toward them. Sociologist and feminist activist Aicha Belarbi finds the scope of INGO actions too limited (e.g., health and literacy programs only) rather than being of general interest to the entire country. Moreover, she says, there are too many INGOs in Morocco, each with a specific small project that often disturbs the work of indigenous organizations rather than helps them; and they often set up their projects without much consultation with the local associations. Finally, Belarbi thinks that INGOS have contributed—along with the state and political parties—to preventing women's associations from developing a unified movement and an effective network of mobilization. Some leaders of Moroccan women's associations have tended to cater to these INGOs for various reasons (access to international funds, prestige, individual visibility, etc.) and have ended up falling into the trap of internal division and competition.

Limits and Potential of Associative Life

Most of the associations mentioned above and others, whose interests are social, cultural, religious, professional, humanitarian, and environmental, comprise, by their very existence, strong constitutive elements of a potential civil society. Indeed, the sheer number and variety of associations mentioned above may give the impression that there is a "vibrant" civil society in Morocco today. Many scholars and politicians do equate this very rich associative map with an actual civil society and refer to it as such. However, if we apply the definition of civil society offered earlier in this book, some key requirements are missing, notably the independence of these associations and their actual participation in, and impact on, public policy.

Given adequate political conditions and a strong political momentum, this associative activity may well develop into the backbone of a real civil society. But this transformation would require persistent and conscious effort on the part of the associations and a genuine political opening on the part of the state. Since associative activity is already a lived practice in Morocco, albeit mostly in the urban centers, the existing associational structures and experience constitute an important advantage in the hands of those social forces seeking both to limit state interference in the private spheres and to affect public policy.

Some of the most important obstacles to this development have been the limitations imposed by a watchful state which wants to maintain its hold on society, and also the limitations imposed by political parties seeking to control civil associations for political purposes. Nadira Bakhkali of the Association Démocratique des Femmes Marocaines indicated in an interview that, for this reason "we created the 'Groupement des ONG' to coordinate the work of associations for the purpose of lobbying for change in the laws that limit associative life in Morocco."[25]

Even though political parties may be considered part of a potential civil society, the relationship that most parties in Morocco have with the monarchy and the state makes them much more an obstacle to, rather than a facilitator of, the transformation of associative life into an actual civil society. This problem is tackled later in this book in the section on political parties and their interaction with the state and the monarchy, on one hand, and with the associations, on the other.

The Independent Press

A free press is an absolute necessity for a democratic environment in which an effective civil society can exist. An independent press serves not only as a medium for civic associations to express their demands and objections, but also as a tool to publicly question and evaluate public policy and to hold office holders accountable.

Even though state control over the independent press has been relaxed in recent years, the Moroccan media remains subject to the same limitations imposed on independent associations. Some 400 newspapers, weeklies, and magazines are published today in Morocco's major cities. These publications range from tabloids to scholarly journals, and from economic magazines to religious periodicals. A large part of the press however, is owned or controlled by either the government or political parties.

In spite of the "self-censorship" phenomenon, which includes avoiding attacks against, or criticism of, the king, Islam, and Morocco's claim to the Western Sahara, the relatively independent press (i.e., the press that does not belong to the government and is not directly controlled by it) has experienced in recent years a slight broadening of its range of action. This relative freedom extends to questioning and criticizing state actions, bureaucratic practices, and the behavior of political leaders (except the king and his close associates), as well as analyzing social, economic, and cultural issues. "Until 1986 we were subjected to censorship before publication. Freedom of expression didn't exist. Now there's a greater margin for maneuvering, but it's somewhat illusory because we have become self-censoring," says Nadir Yata, editor of the daily *Al-Bayane*.[26]

Under Article 55 of the Press Code, the government has the power to censor newspapers and to order them not to report on specific events or issues. It is worth noting, however, that while the state still exercises vigilant control over the press and can seize a given issue before its distribution, it rarely suspends a publication outright.

The written press is accessible to less than half of the population because of the still very high level of adult illiteracy in Morocco (59.9 percent in 1994), and much of it caters to the educated middle class and the urban elite. In contrast to the relative progress in the freedom of action of the written press, television and radio journalism remains tightly controlled. Audio/visual journalism, accessible to illiterate and literate alike, provides mostly an officially-sanctioned version of facts and events and serves as the main medium for the relay of official ideology.

The condition of Morocco's television and radio press is similar to those found in Algeria and Tunisia, where the broadcast media have always been controlled by the state. In these two countries, however, a relatively independent written press was allowed to develop in the 1980s and, in Algeria, in part of the 1990s. But in both Algeria and Tunisia, this independent written press progressively lost much of its freedom as a result of political developments. In Tunisia, the crackdown against the Islamists in the late 1980s, and later against most opposition groups, inhibited press freedom almost entirely. In Algeria, the sudden and radical opening of the political system in the late 1980s—after major youth riots in October 1988—allowed the birth and development of an independent written press that enjoyed an almost unique freedom of expression in the Maghrib, but for a few years only.

In the wake of the struggle between the state and a radicalized Islamist movement, both the Islamists and the state targeted newspapers and journalists they did not agree with. Dozens of journalists were assassinated by Islamist groups from 1993 to 1997 and many others were arrested, or their newspapers were shut down by the state. By early 1998, state bureaucracies in all three countries held the press on a tight leash; relative press freedom had become once again contingent upon institutionalized "self-censorship" and on political conjunctures that either tolerated or muted free expression in the name of national security.

In Morocco many press leaders indicate today that freedom of expression has broadened in recent years, but they also contend that much remains to be done in order to allow society to freely evaluate and challenge governmental actions and policies.

The development of a truly free press is, of course, one of the most important prerequisites of civil society and must be part of any process of genuine democratization. Moreover, an independent and free press provides an important outlet for the expression of societal desires and grievances. If this outlet is too limited or is nonexistent, people turn to street rioting—or even to armed rebellion as in the case of Algeria—as the only way to express displeasure with a given situation or policy. The lack of such an outlet certainly contributed to social unrest in Morocco throughout the 1980s and in the early 1990s.

Notes

1. Abdallah Saaf, "L'Hypothèse de la Société Civile au Maroc," in Noureddine El-Aoufi, ed., *La Société Civile au Maroc* (Rabat, Morocco: Societé Marocaine des Editeurs Réunis, 1992), p. 13.

2. For an insightful discussion on the private sector in Morocco, see Abdelkader Berrada and Mohamed Said Saadi, "Le Grand Capital Privé Marocain," in Jean-Claude Santucci, ed., *Le Maroc Actuel: Une Modernisation au Miroir de la Tradition?* (Paris: CNRS, 1992), pp. 325-391.

3. For an interesting insight into these networks, see Ali Benhaddou, *Maroc: Les Elites du Royaume: Essai sur l'Organisation du Pouvoir au Maroc* (Paris: Editions L'Harmattan, 1997), especially the chapter "Les Marriages et les Affaires" (marriages and business).

4. Mark A. Tessler and John P. Entelis, "Kingdom of Morocco," in David E. Long and Bernard Reich, eds., *The Government and Politics of the Middle East and North Africa* (Boulder, CO: Westview Press, 1986), p. 403.

5. Fathallah Oulaâlou, Interview, Rabat, Morocco, July 1994.

6. Abderrahim Lamchichi, *Islam et la Contestation au Maghreb* (Paris: Editions L'Harmattan, 1989), pp. 122-125.

7. For an extensive list of *Da'wa* associations in Morocco, see François Burgat and William Dowell, *The Islamic Movement in North Africa* (Austin, TX: Center for Middle Eastern Studies, University of Texas, 1997), p. 170.

8. Abdelkrim Moutii has been living in exile —probably in Belgium —since December 1975, right after the assassination of Omar Ben Jalloun who was the editor of the socialist newspaper *Al-Muharrir* and one of the most prominent Marxist intellectuals in Morocco. The government accused Moutii's Jam'iyat al-Shabiba al-Islamiyya of having committed his murder. See Henry Munson, *Religion and Power in Morocco* (New Haven, CT: Yale University Press, 1993), pp.160-161.

9. For a succinct discussion of the *Shurafa*, see A. Agnouche, "Les Charfa Face à l' 'Etat de Droit' dans le Maroc Contemporain," in Jean-Claude Santucci, ed., *Le Maroc Actuel: Une Modernisation au Miroir de la Tradition?* (Paris: CNRS, 1992), 273-283. The word *shurafa* is the plural of *sharif* which refers to the idea of "rising," or "to go beyond." With regard to individuals, it refers to the "free man who, thanks to his glorious ancestry [the *shurafa* of the Hassanides and the Husseinides dynasties of the 8th century] can claim a predominant status" (p. 275-276). The *Shurafa*, who claim descent from the prophet Mohamed, have a social-political function and several important privileges, including not being liable before a court of law, and not having to pay taxes. In the 1960s, the *Shurafa* organized in the form of a *Rabita*, or confederation of associations, for the purpose of defending their interests. In order to counterbalance the rising power of the *Rabita* and to put a stop to the number of people claiming to be of a *Shurafa* lineage, King Hassan, starting in 1979, established around 100 *Nuqaba* (plural of *Naqib*) as a parallel set of associations to represent the *Shurafa*. Today's *Shurafa* include such families as the Kettani, Ouazzani, Idrissi, Alaoui, and Amrani (Claisse, "Makhzen Aujourd'hui," in Santucci, ed., *Le Maroc Actuel*, p. 303).

10. The 1994 armed attack in Marrakesh and the ensuing court trials of people linked to it indicate the potential radicalization of the Moroccan Islamist movement, especially in concert with other Islamist networks in the Maghrib and Europe.

11. The Algerian party formerly called Hamas is not associated with the Palestinian movement of the same name. They use very different political discourses and present

different views on the means to pursue their respective objectives. The Algerian Hamas rejects violence as a political means while the Palestinian Hamas justifies its use against Israeli occupation. The names of Hamas and al-Nahda al-Islamiyya were changed to comply with the November 1996 constitutional amendment in Algeria which required parties to remove from their names any reference to Islam.

12. Abderrahim Lamchichi, "Les incertitudes politiques et sociales: L'islamism s'enracine au Maroc," *Le Monde Diplomatique*, May 1996, pp. 10-11.

13. Ibid.

14. Emad Eldin Shahin, "Secularism and Nationalism: The Political Discourse of 'Abd al-Salam Yassin," in John Ruedy, ed., *Islamism and Secularism in North Africa* (New York: St. Martin Press, 1996), p. 184.

15. Joel Donnet, "Après deux milles ans de mépris, renaissance berbère au Maroc," *Le Monde Diplomatique*, January 1995, p. 18.

16. Three members of the Tilelli association were arrested in Goulmima and were sentenced to up to two years in jail for "disturbing the peace" because they carried a banner during the Labor Day parade calling for Tamazight to be made an official language. An appeals court reduced their sentences and the king pardoned them in July, when 424 political prisoners were freed.

17. Donnet, "Après deux milles ans de mépris," op. cit, p 18.

18. George Sabagh, "The Challenge of Population Growth in Morocco," *Middle East Report* 23:2, March-April 1993, p. 33.

19. Aicha Belarbi, "Mouvements des Femmes au Maroc," in Noureddine El-Aoufi, ed., *La Société Civile au Maroc* (Rabat, Morocco: Societé Marocaine des Editeurs Réunis, 1992), p. 185.

20. Ibid.

21. John P. Entelis, *Comparative Politics of North Africa: Algeria, Morocco and Tunisia* (New York: Syracuse University Press, 1980), p. 75.

22. For example, Habib al-Malki, an economist and active member of the opposition party USFP, was recruited as head of the CNJA in 1990.

23. Hakima Himmich and Latifa, Imane, "Les ONG au Maroc, Pour Une Société Civile à l'Identité Plurielle: Le Cas de l'Association Marocaine de Lutte Contre Le SIDA," paper presented at Atelier Maghrebin de Réflection: Quelles Actions Solidaires Pour un Développement Durable au Maghreb? Le Role des ONG, Rabat, Morocco, July 2-4, 1993, p. 1. (Translation mine.)

24. Ibid., p. 2.

25. Nadira Bakhkali, Interview, Rabat, July 11, 1994.

26. Nadir Yata, editor of the French-language daily *Al-Bayane* (of the PPS party), Interview in Barbara Borst, "Progress Toward Democracy or Window Dressing?" *Inter Press Service* (IPS), May 29, 1995. (Translation mine.)

VII

Political Parties and Civil Society

Many leaders of opposition parties in Morocco speak of civil society as a necessary condition for a democratic change in Morocco. For them, clearly, the mere existence of the associations with which they deal on a regular basis does not indicate in itself that a civil society already exists. Yet in spite of their wish for a genuine civil society in which independent associations would be central, they often interact with existing associations in a utilitarian and opportunist fashion. They encourage their party members to join certain groups in order to make sure that the objectives and principles of the party are promoted in and by these organizations. They tend to officially court these associations mostly at election time.

There does not seem to be, therefore, a sustained or conscious effort by most opposition parties to encourage these associations to be instrumental in the birth of a civil society which would be independent from the state and which could serve as an arena for the promotion of partisan interests when they coincide with the interests of any group in society.

There are approximately 28 political parties in Morocco, with varying degrees of appeal and importance. They are all supportive of the monarchical regime, and perform a function of opposition that is less confrontational than that observed in truly open and competitive polities. Multiparty politics in Morocco predates independence and has not been incompatible with the monarchical system of government. In fact, multiparty politics in Morocco has reinforced the power of the monarchy by encouraging division among the opposition and by giving the king the image of a political figure who transcends conflicting party politics and unifies the nation. As "a tool to neutralize the parties that came out of the national movement [for independence], multipartism became an essential dimension of a regime characterized by the political monopoly of the throne."[1]

The representation of political currents has a meaning only in so far as it primarily helps in the control of these currents by those in power; the expression of political parties, which goes as far as a recognition of the opposition, is always carefully conditioned by the acceptance of a political pact which could neither question the essential principles of the regime, nor influence its fundamental equilibria.[2]

Since independence, the monarchy has manipulated the party configurations by including some parties in the management of the affairs of the state, excluding others, repressing some, and even promoting the birth of a pro-monarchy bloc which would dominate parliamentary life, when there was one. In fact, the "Moroccan system of client-patron relationships reproduces itself in the political parties, which are more or less clients."[3]

Rather than constituting a united front to counterbalance the domineering monarchical and state powers, opposition parties often clash with each other in fierce political battles. However, in a few instances, some of the major opposition parties have formed temporary tactical alliances, such as the five-party alliance called Koutla during the 1993 parliamentary elections. But such alliances tend to be fragile or short-lived. The 1993 Koutla included the Istiqlal party, the National Union of Popular Forces (UNFP), the Socialist Union of Popular Forces (USFP), the Party of Progress and Socialism (PPS), and the Organization of Democratic and Popular Action (OADP).

Moroccan scholar Abdelkader El Benna points out that "it is very difficult in this context to link the proliferation of political parties to democracy or to equate multipartism with political pluralism."[4] Nevertheless, this limited pluralism is almost unique in the Arab world and may serve as a sound basis for the development of a genuine multiparty polity. The old tradition of multipartism in Morocco—albeit controlled and even co-opted—offers the benefit of institutionalized processes of interaction among the parties themselves, and between them, society, and the state. Below is an overview of the genesis and nature of some of these parties.

The Istiqlal Party was founded in 1943 as a nationalist movement for independence. It is formally committed to a tolerant Islam which it recognizes as an important source of Morocco's social, political, and cultural values. It "represents a traditional, defensive, and status-quo oriented segment of a small urban and rural population, with traditional strongholds in Fez and Meknès."[5] The Istiqlal party remains provincial and has strong support among peasants, landowners, commercial interests, and women. It has always supported the monarchy, but on occasion it reiterates a call for the establishment of a truly constitutional monarchy in which it hopes to participate in governing the country. Since the days of the national movement against colonialism, the Istiqlal party has had a special relationship with the monarchy. They need each other for legitimacy and political viability. If post-independence Morocco had opted for a one-party system, the Istiqlal party would probably have been that party.

Like the other parties in Morocco, the Istiqlal has been torn, since independence, by major internal divisions and discord which have weakened it and made it often appear to support the status quo rather than change and opposition. The biggest internal division happened in 1959 when leftist elements within the party dissented and created the UNFP, which is more confrontational. The Istiqlal party has been headed by M'hamed Boucetta since 1974.

The National Union of Popular Forces (UNFP) was created in 1959 by a group of former Istiqlal members led by Mehdi Ben Barka. It started out as a highly combative leftist, nationalist, and trade-unionist movement. It did not intend to become a party; it started rather as a simple effort to boost the nationalist and the leftist tendencies within the Istiqlal. In the end, the effort turned into a new party that accepted the monarchical regime while maintaining a revolutionary orientation. For a long time, the UNFP was torn between two opposing tendencies: the revolutionary urge to conquer power by all means, including armed struggle, and the democratic path to acquiring or sharing power. One section of the party leadership was willing to work with the king, while the other rejected any cooperation with him.

Lacking clarity about both its objectives and the means to achieve them, and unable to cater to both the petite bourgeoisie and the working class, both of which it claimed as its social basis, the UNFP fell into an identity crisis in the mid-1960s which played into the hands of the monarchy and the other opposition parties. It never fully recovered from this crisis and the disappearance of its leader in 1965 (allegedly abducted and assassinated in France) further weakened the party. State repression and internal dissent and division contributed to its decline. Finally, a group of members broke away in 1972 and created the USFP which was to become a strong party of the left. Today, the weak UNFP includes in its ranks trade-unionists, former resistance fighters, and some leftist nationalists.

The Socialist Union of Popular Forces (USFP) was founded after the 1972 rift within the UNFP and quickly became the second most important party after the Istiqlal. From the outset, the USFP committed itself to acquiring power through elections, building socialism, and establishing a socialist democracy. It accepts liberal democracy only as a necessary stage for capturing power. Its immediate mission is to press for a democratic opening of the political system and to play an active and revolutionary role in that system. In practice, however, the party finds itself too close to the system it is pledged to change. Though subdued by repression, the USFP remains a source of potential challenge to the monarch. It attracts urban youth, especially those in high schools and universities, civil servants, and members of the liberal professions. It is headed today by Abderrahmane Youssoufi, who returned to Morocco in 1995 after a short period of self-exile overseas. He was appointed prime minister on February 4, 1998.

The Party of Progress and Socialism (PPS) was formed in 1968 by members of the banned Moroccan Communist Party. Prior to 1974, it was known as the Party of Liberation and Socialism. Before it was allowed to exist as a party, the PPS had to move from the far left to the center, thereby compromising its revolutionary line. The party's tactics have included the mobilization of the masses for the purpose of taking power by democratic means. However, it has been unable to mobilize the working class, as it set out to do. To many people, the PPS, which is headed by Ali Yata, seems to have spent more energy courting the throne than courting its constituency.

The Organization of Democratic and Popular Action (OADP) was formed in 1983 by former members of the USFP and the PPS. Originally known as the Marxist-Leninist Movement or MML, this party was at first driven by revolutionary zeal. In the long run and after having been repressed, the MML opted for a democratic path to socialism and changed its name to the OADP. Not able to develop the large social base it claims to have among the working class, and not trusted by the state and the throne because of its radical past, the OADP competes in vain for leadership of the Moroccan left. It has also not been able to become part of the "system" as have the more established traditional parties such as the Istiqlal and the USFP. Under the leadership of Mohamed Bensaid Ait Idder, the OADP opposed the constitutional reform of September 1996. Its call for a "no" vote caused it to be excluded from all official regional and national activities. This legal ban, which originated in the Interior Ministry and was lifted in January 1997 by a royal decision, closed down most party activities, including the party publication. An application for permission to publish a new publication has been put on hold indefinitely by the state. Moreover, this party suffered yet another important blow when some of its members decided to pull out and form a rival party, the Socialist Democratic Party (PSD). The young PSD managed to obtain control of 9 municipalities in the local elections of June 13, 1997 and 9 seats in the parliamentary elections of November, while the OADP received 11 and 4 respectively.

The National Rally of Independents (RNI) was formed by a parliamentary group in 1977 and is often referred to as "a party of the monarchy" because of its close links to the throne and its appeal to the high bureaucratic elite and bourgeoisie. It is committed to the monarchical regime and to democratic principles and has been trying, since its creation, to establish itself as an independent and respectable party. In practice, this remains a difficult task for the RNI, which is headed by Ahmed Osman, a former prime minister and the king's brother-in-law.

The National Democratic Party (PND) was founded in 1981 by former members of the RNI (led by Arsalane al-Jadidi) and is a pro-monarchy formation. Claiming to be carrying on the true mission of the RNI, this party declares itself the representative of the peasantry. In practice, the PND is close to the state and the monarchy and seems to have no independent line.

The Constitutional Union (UC) is a moderate party that was created in 1983 by former prime minister Maati Bouabid. It enjoys support from the king and promotes the idea of national unity and identity around the monarchy. It supports economic and political liberalism and views both Islam and the monarchy as fundamental constituents of Morocco's identity. Like the RNI, this party remains closely linked to the throne and the high bureaucratic elite. To many of its rivals in Morocco, it is no more than an election-minded congregation of conservative elements. In fact, the party now quite often shows signs of life between elections. After the death of Bouabid on November 1, 1996, and in the absence of a strong heir to the president's office, the party established a collective leadership of 13 members ("groupe de gestion et de suivi") who will alternate as party presidents until the party congress elects the new leader.

The Popular Movement (MP) is an Amazigh-based, monarchist party that was created in 1957. It came about as a strong opposition group to the Istiqlal party and has maintained its anti-Istiqlal stance. It also has served to contain the Amazigh movement by offering it an officially-condoned framework of action. The MP promotes an Islamic socialism and the recognition of the strong and distinct Amazigh characteristics of Morocco. It is a staunch supporter of the monarchy, though it calls for a constitutional monarchy. Currently, it has a very weak standing among the opposition—because of its very close association with the throne—and is badly torn by internal conflict over issues and political strategy.

Several other parties exist and have participated in electoral competitions, such as the municipal and parliamentary elections of 1992, 1993, and 1997. Among them are the Mouvement Démocratique et Social (Democratic and Social Movement, MDS); the Mouvement National Populaire (National Popular Movement, MNP) and the Mouvement Populaire Démocratique et Constitutionel (Popular Democratic and Constitutional Movement, MPDC), which are splinter groups of the MP; the Parti d'Action (Action Party, PA), established by Amazigh intellectuals; and the Parti Démocratique d'Indépendants (Democratic Party of Independents, PDI).

The very rich landscape of political parties described above constitutes a clear indicator of Morocco's multipartism. There is a wide variety of views on several issues that set many parties apart from each other and there are also perspectives shared by most of them, such as those on the Western Sahara and the role of monarchy. However, this multipartism has yet to turn into an actual political pluralism which allows the formulation and articulation of views that stray from the mainstream (i.e., conformist) current. Moreover, the inability of political parties to act as a counterbalance to the powers of both the monarchy and the state apparatus has directly affected the power of associations to do so. As emphasized earlier, many associations are directly or indirectly controlled by parties and find their scope of interest articulation and action limited to what the system and the parties allow. One of the main causes of this situation, as the next section shows, has been a strong resistance of the monarchy and the state to the emergence of political pluralism because such pluralism threatens the power configuration and the status quo.

Notes

1. Michel Camau, "Pouvoir et Institutions au Maghreb," (Cérès Production, 1978), p. 81, cited in Abdelkader El Benna, "Les Partis Politiques au Maroc," in Noureddine El-Aoufi, ed., *La Société Civile au Maroc* (Rabat, Morocco: Societé Marocaine des Editeurs Réunis, 1992), p. 130. (Translation mine).

2. Jean-Claude Santucci, "Etat et Société au Maroc: Enjeux et Perspectives du Changement," in Jean-Claude Santucci, ed., *Le Maroc Actuel: Une Modernisation au Miroir de la Tradition?* (Paris: CNRS, 1992), p. 428. (Translation mine).

3. Bassam Tibi, *Islam and the Cultural Accommodation of Social Change* (Boulder, CO: Westview Press, 1991), p. 170.

4. Abdelkader El Benna, "Les Partis Politiques au Maroc," in Noureddine El-Aoufi, ed., *La Société Civile au Maroc* (Rabat, Morocco: Societé Marocaine des Editeurs Réunis, 1992), p. 130 (Translation mine).

5. John P. Entelis, *Comparative Politics of North Africa: Algeria, Morocco and Tunisia* (New York: Syracuse University Press, 1980), p. 70.

VIII

Limits of Political Reforms and Elections in the 1990s

In the 1990s, there were two major electoral events in Morocco. Each one promised to move the country into an era of true democracy. The first, which took place in 1993, failed badly to do so and, instead, pushed Morocco into a deep political malaise. The second, which took place in 1997, did not challenge some of the existing patterns but did introduce some hopeful changes, notably the appointment of the opposition leader as prime minister. To make a significant change, it took a constitutional amendment in 1996 which reformed the voting system and restructured parliament. The importance and consequences of these events must be examined in order to highlight both the limitations embedded in the system and the potential for a genuine break from the status quo.

The Parliamentary Elections of 1993

After having been deferred for many years, Morocco's two-stage parliamentary elections were finally held on June 25 and September 17, 1993. The whole process was open to inspection by the opposition and by international observers. In the first round, two-thirds of a 333-member parliament (that is, 222) were elected by direct universal suffrage, while in the second round, three months later, the remaining one-third (111) was elected indirectly by electoral colleges of communal councils, professional chambers, and labor unions. The communal councils had to fill 69 seats, the Chamber of Agriculture 15, the Chamber of Commerce and Industry 10, the Chamber of Craftspeople 7, and the Chamber of Labor Unions 10.

In the first round, the opposition obtained very good results, but in the second round it performed badly. Whereas the results of the first vote gave great hope to the opposition, those of the second deceived it. In the first round, the USFP obtained 48 seats and the Istiqlal 43, but in the second round they received only 4 and 7, respectively (see Table 1). For the pro-government formations, the proportions were quite different: the MP received 33 in the first round and 18 in the second; the CU received 27 in both rounds, and the RNI had 28 in the first and 13 in the second.

Altogether, the opposition coalition, the Koutla, consisting of the PI, USFP, PPS and the OADP, obtained 99 seats (out of 222) in the first ballot and only 15 (out of 111) in the second, while the previous pro-government majority (MP, UC, RNI, MNP, PND) received 116 seats in the first and 79 in the second round. The Koutla opposition found the disproportion between the results of the two rounds unacceptable and denounced what it asserted were electoral manipulations. The inconsistency was thought to have resulted from electoral tampering by the government and its allied parties. Because of this purported deception, the opposition refused to take part in the new government and asked for an investigation of the second vote.[1]

The end result of these elections was that no single party or group of parties controlled a majority of seats; this was viewed by the opposition as a deliberate manipulation by the king in order to avoid facing a majority that could effectively use the newly-reinforced powers of parliament. The great hope in the summer of 1993 that Morocco was on the verge of changing its political map thanks to greater participation by opposition parties suddenly dissipated and things seemed to revert back to the status quo ante.

This electoral outcome threw the political system into a crisis, and a general malaise ensued among the political elite. The International Foundation for Electoral Systems, which sent a team of observers during the June elections, reported no major problems and published a report which expressed general satisfaction with the process. It did not comment on the September elections and simply mentioned that their results were seriously challenged by the opposition.[2]

The crisis that followed the elections was characterized first, by a sharp dispute among opposition leaders on whether or not to ac-

PARTIES & UNIONS	1984 Total Results	6/25/93 Results	9/17/93 Results	1993 Total Results
TABLE 1: THE 1984 AND 1993 PARLIAMENTARY ELECTIONS[3]				
PARTIES OF THE PRE-1993 MAJORITY				
Popular Movement (MP)	31	33	18	51
Constitutional Union (UC)	56	27	27	54
National Rally of Independents (RNI)	39	28	13	41
National Popular Movement (MNP)	----	14	11	25
National Democratic Party (PND)	15	14	10	24
TOTAL	**141**	**116**	**79**	**195**
PARTIES OF KOUTLA (OPPOSITIONAL ALLIANCE)				
Socialist Union of Popular Forces (USFP)	35	48	4	52
Istiqlal Party (PI)	24	43	7	50
Party of Progress and Socialism (PPS)	2	6	4	10
Org. of Democratic & Popular Action	1	2	0	2
TOTAL	**62**	**99**	**15**	**114**
OTHERS				
Party of Shoura and Independence	–	3	6	9
Action Party (PA)	–	2	–	2
Democratic Labor Confederation (CDT)	–	–	4	4
Moroccan Union of Workers	–	–	3	3
General Union of Moroccan Workers	–	–	2	2
Independent Candidates	–	2	2	4
TOTAL	–	7	17	24
TOTAL FOR 1993 ELECTIONS		**222**		**333**

cept the September results and a token participation in the government, and, second, by a deep crisis within the USFP. However, in spite of serious divisions within and between opposition parties, the USFP and the Istiqlal parties agreed at least on refusing to participate in any new government unless they were given certain key ministerial posts—including those of the Interior and Justice ministries.

The party that was hardest hit by internal division was the USFP. A few days after the September election results were announced, Abderrahmane Youssoufi, the secretary general of the party, resigned and left for France, where he stayed until Spring 1995. Mohamed al-Yazghi, the first deputy secretary general, became the temporary *de facto* leader, but the party refused to make any major decision in the absence of its secretary general. Youssoufi agreed with the USFP faction that believes that the system can be changed from within, that is, through a compromise-based participation of the socialists in the elections and in the government. However, the alleged manipulations of the 1993 elections strengthened the position of another faction which believed in holding out for a real change in the system. This faction rejected all invitations to participate in the government or to compromise with the powers that be; it believed that the longer the opposition held out, the more likely the system would feel pressured to change. Youssoufi, who had been willing to work within the system, felt greatly deceived when that same system failed to deliver on its promise of openness. When he abandoned the leadership of the party, he indirectly acknowledged that the "rejectionist" faction of his party was right.

Youssoufi was not the only USFP leader to be absent from the country. Mohamed Basri (known as the *Faqih*) had left Morocco some 30 years earlier and was condemned to death three times for his outright opposition. Basri had made his return conditional on major changes in the human rights policy of Morocco. The absence of these two leaders made it even more difficult for the USFP to maintain discipline and unity among its ranks and to formulate an unambiguous position vis-à-vis the electoral results and their aftermath.

Following the parliamentary vote of 1993, the king extended the term of Prime Minister Mohamed Karim Lamrani who had held that office since August 11, 1992. His government had been expected at that time to be temporary and to only help with the transition to a political configuration based on the 1993 elections results.

But after the opposition refused to partake in any post-election government, Lamrani was retained as prime minister until May 25, 1994 when the king replaced him with the highly respected foreign minister, Abdellatif Filali. It was hoped that because he was respected as a technocrat, i.e., as a man above partisan cleavages, Filali might be able to draw in the opposition's cooperation and participation. He did not succeed in doing so. The USFP and the Istiqlal, among others, stood firm in their positions. In the spring of 1995, Filali, who had also retained his foreign minister post, formed a second government of technocrats. The opposition's boycott only deepened the malaise among the Moroccan political community, which was already burdened by the worsening economic situation (negative growth rate and increasing social and economic inequalities). At that point, not only the opposition but also the king himself wished that USFP leaders Youssoufi and Basri would return from self-exile and help end the political deadlock. Many people expected Basri would bring unity to the opposition, including the Islamists.[4] When Basri and Youssoufi finally returned to Morocco in 1995, however, the two leaders managed neither to reunite their party nor to lead the opposition in a coordinated strategy for the 1997 municipal and parliamentary elections.

The constitutional reform of 1996 and the parliamentary elections of fall 1997 offered the theoretical possibility of a future Koutla-controlled parliament, but the results of these elections fell short. However, both the 1996 reform of parliament and the 1997 elections carried some potential for a more active role of the opposition in government and public policy. In fact, the results of the 1997 parliamentary vote put the USFP in a position of possible leadership in a new government but not necessarily with the full support of all of its Koutla allies. The main electoral ally of the USFP, the Istiqlal, expressed strong reservations about participating in the government because of its unhappiness with the results of these elections.

Constitutional Reform of 1996

Reflecting a desire to end the deadlock that had gripped Moroccan politics since the 1993 elections, a referendum on major constitutional reform relating to the structure and election of parliament was held on September 13, 1996. Popular debate on the reform took place just after a turbulent spring characterized by a series of strikes and even a riot in Tangier on June 5, 1996. The constitutional reform abolished the indirect vote for part of the Assembly (renamed House of Representatives) and established an upper house called the Chamber of Counselors to be filled by representatives of local councils, professional bodies, and trade unions. The House of Representatives is filled by direct popular vote. In this reorganization of parliament, the Chamber of Counselors can alone censure the government and force a shuffling of the king's appointed Cabinet. There was hope, however, that the new institutional arrangement would allow the opposition to control the lower house of the legislative body and the government if it were to win enough seats in the next legislative elections.

The Municipal Elections of 1997

The Koutla obtained better results in the municipal elections of June 13, 1997, than in the parliamentary vote that followed. As Table 2 shows, the number of municipalities controlled by the Koutla parties (PI, OADP, PPS and USFP) jumped from 219 in the 1992 elections to 405 in 1997. Within this group, the Istiqlal party improved its lot by 50 percent (from 147 in 1992 to 221), the USFP doubled the number of municipalities it controlled (from 68 to 139) while the PPS multiplied by more than eight times the number of local offices it held (from 4 to 34); the OADP, which had boycotted the 1992 vote, obtained control of 11 municipalities in 1997.

The pro-government formations generally did not perform well, with the exception of the Popular Movement (MP) which improved its lot by 10 percent by obtaining the control of 234 municipalities. The RNI's control went down from 378 municipalities to 251, the UC down from 248 to 214, the PND decreased from 118 to 85, and the MNP down from 166 to 72 municipalities. The new party of Mahmoud Archane, the Democratic and Social Movement (MDS, born in 1996), surprised everyone by obtaining the control of 112 municipalities and 33 seats in the new parliament (fifth in ranking). The MDS rejects the allegation that it is a "pro-administration" party, espouses most of the demands and slogans of the Koutla and presents itself as a social-democratic party of the center.

Even though the opposition parties of the Koutla almost doubled the number of municipalities they controlled, their overall standing

TABLE 2: 1992 AND 1997 MUNICIPAL ELECTIONS[5]		
PARTIES	1992 Elections	1997 Elections
PARTIES OF THE RIGHT (PRO-GOVERNMENT)		
Constitutional Union (UC)	248	214
National Democratic Party (PND)	118	85
Popular Movement (MP)	212	234
TOTAL	**578**	**533**
PARTIES OF KOUTLA (OPPOSITIONAL ALLIANCE)		
Istiqlal Party (PI)	147	221
Organization of Democractic and Popular Action (OADP)	-	11
Party of Progress and Socialism (PPS)	4	34
Socialist Union of Popular Forces (USFP)	68	139
TOTAL	**219**	**405**
CENTER (NEW)		
National Popular Movement (MNP)	166	72
National Rally of Independents (RNI)	378	251
Democratic and Social Movement (MDS)	–	112
TOTAL	**544**	**435**

still lags behind that of the other party blocs. As indicated by Table 2, the pro-government formations and those referred to nowadays as the Center, control respectively 533 and 435, that is, 968 municipalities out of 1,517.

Despite the relative importance of the opposition's gain in these elections, they are not likely to change the political map of Morocco. To many Moroccans, this vote has been nothing more than a confirmation of the overall status quo.[6] Hope of change had been placed not only in the parliamentary elections, but in the empowerment of parliament and the opposition parties to make public policies with a direct, immediate, and positive impact on people's lives.

The Parliamentary Elections of 1997

The parliamentary elections of November 14, 1997, brought no substantial change to the existing political map of Morocco, except for the emergence of an informal center bloc and the appointment of an opposition leader, Youssoufi, as prime minister. In spite of the relative gains of the Koutla parties and the absence of a majority-controlling party or bloc of parties, most seats have, in fact, remained in the hand of "pro-administration" and pro-monarchy parties.

The reshuffling of political parties into three major blocs (a leftist Koutla, a rightist Wifaq, and a social-democratic center) did not alter the power structure. This new party configuration replaces the previous two-bloc set-up (opposition versus pro-government formations) but most seats remain in the hands of pro-establishment parties of the Wifaq and center blocs. All three party blocs, the Koutla, the Wifaq and the center, received an almost equal number of seats each (102, 100 and 97, respectively).

The party that won most seats in the lower house was the USFP, which obtained 57 seats, followed by the UC with 50 seats and the RNI with 46 seats. In the upper house, however, the RNI has the highest number of seats, 37, followed by the new party, the MDS, with 33 seats, and the UC and MP with 25 seats each. As Table 3 indicates, the total numbers of seats obtained in both houses were 247 for the center parties, 169 for the Wifaq group and 143 for the Koutla alliance, out of a total of 595 seats (325 in the House of Representatives and 270 in the Chamber of Counselors).

It is interesting to note that, in these elections, there were important disproportions between gains in the two houses. The Wifaq group obtained 100 seats in the lower house and 69 in the upper house, and the Center parties received 97 and 84 in the respective houses.

The Koutla, which had received 102 seats in the lower house, obtained merely 41 in the upper house. In the House of Representatives, the PI won only 32 seats while its alliance partner the USFP received 57, making it the first party in that house. Just as in the 1993 elections, both parties complained about these elections, claim-

Parties and Party Blocs	1993 Totals	1997 House of Reps.	1997 Chamber of Counselors	1997 Total Parliament
TABLE 3: 1993 AND 1997 PARLIAMENTARY ELECTIONS[7]				
PARTIES OF THE WIFAQ (RIGHT)				
Constitutional Union (UC)	54	50	25	75
National Democratic Party (PND)	24	10	19	29
Popular Movement (MP)	51	40	25	65
TOTAL	**129**	**100**	**69**	**169**
PARTIES OF KOUTLA (OPPOSITION/LEFT)				
Istiqlal Party (PI)	50	32	19	51
Organization of Democratic and Popular Action (OADP)	2	4	-	4
Party of Progress and Socialism (PPS)	10	9	7	16
Socialist Union of Popular Forces (USFP)	52	57	15	72
TOTAL	**114**	**102**	**41**	**143**
CENTER PARTIES				
National Popular Movement (MNP)	25	19	14	33
National Rally of Independents (RNI)	41	46	37	83
Democratic and Social Movement (MDS)	-	32	33	62
TOTAL	**66**	**97**	**84**	**247**
OTHER PARTIES				
Popular Democratic and Constitutional Movement (MPDC)	-	9	-	9
Socialist Democratic Party (PSD)	-	5	4	9
Front of Democratic Forces (FFD)	-	9	-	9

ing that the results were again manipulated. However, only the Istiqlal Party took a radical position and demanded their cancellation, while the USFP toned down its criticism in the hope of obtaining the control of the future government. The fragile Koutla alliance suffered when the Istiqlal Party announced that it might refuse to take part in any future government, whereas the USFP, under the leadership of Youssoufi, seemed ready to join a coalition government in which it hoped to control the office of prime minister.

As expected by most observers, the leader of the USFP, Youssoufi, was appointed prime minister by the king on February 4, 1998. This appointment seemed to respond to two rationales: the first was the fact that the USFP deserved such privilege because it had won the largest number of seats in the lower house of parliament, and second, such an appointment would definitely indicate a substantial departure from previous patterns of appointment of prime ministers. A major opposition party has finally become a governing party, breaking a tradition of pro-monarchy heads of government. Of course, such an appointment cannot be considered actual change in the Moroccan political practice and mechanisms. When foreign minister Abdellatif Filali was appointed as a non-partisan prime minister in 1994 a lot of hope was placed in his potential ability to effect such change. During his tenure in office, however, nothing changed. This explains in part people's apathy regarding the last elections and the appointment of the new prime minister. Skepticism will certainly continue to reign until substantial reform takes place in the political process and in public policies. In order for the prime minister to begin fulfilling some of the hopes placed in the recent institutional reforms and personnel appointments, he must first mobilize a stable coalition of supporters within both houses of parliament, and, second, King Hassan must allow him some leeway in taking innovative initiatives that could help deal with some of the most important problems faced by Morocco today (e.g., poverty, corruption, injustice). It would be difficult for Youssoufi to challenge the pillars of structural adjustment even though some of them may well be the sources of the grave social and economic dislocations that have resulted from the reforms enacted since the early 1980s. Resistance to him may come not only from the monarchy itself but also from individuals in the business sector and in state institutions whose benefits are best served by the status quo.

While the effects of the parliamentary vote of 1997 and the appointment of an opposition leader as prime minister are still unfolding and their real consequences are yet to be known, some important observations can already be made.

First, the elections results of 1997 were not as contested as those of 1993, even though there were reports of some illegal practices; in general, the pact signed by the king and the parties for fair elections and respect of their results held out in the end.

Second, Morocco's party configuration is today more diverse than before; instead of two major blocs, there are now three (left, right and center), plus a few independent parties. Since the 1993 elections at least two new parties have been born. This has divided further the party map, which is in the interest of the monarchy since it still has apprehensions about the potential challenge of a united bloc of parties with a majority control in parliament.

Third, for the first time, Islamist candidates were allowed to enter parliament. The moderate Islamist party, the Popular Democratic and Constitutional Movement (MPDC) was permitted to take part in these elections and to accept that members of Harakat al-Tawhid wa al-Islah (Movement of Unity and Reform) run under its name. Altogether, the Islamists now have nine representatives in the lower house of parliament.

Fourth, the Koutla alliance (known also as the "democratic bloc") came out of this election year very divided. Strong tensions continue between and within the parties of the alliance regarding the political strategy to follow. Between the two major parties, the USFP and Istiqlal, a new tension has arisen because of the Istiqlal's rejection of electoral results and refusal to cooperate with the USFP on a coalition government made up of elements from the Koutla and small parties of the left and center. Moreover, the other two Koutla parties, the OADP and the PPS, also suffered an important setback after some of their members decided to form their own parties and run independently in the elections. The new Socialist Democratic Party (PSD) came out of the OADP and the new Front of Democratic Forces (FFD) came out of the PPS (see Table 3). In spite of the relative gains made by some members of the Koutla, the 1997 electoral year witnessed the weakening of this "democratic bloc." Even with the USFP controlling the largest number of seats in the lower house and the office of prime minister, power in parliament still rests in the hands of the six parties of the Wifaq (UC, PND, MP) and the center (MNP, RNI, MDS) which are known for leaning in favor of the administration and the monarchy in spite of their claims otherwise.

The recent political developments discussed above carry two opposing prospects for the future: they may usher in a gradual but moderate change in the political practice in Morocco, or they may have no real effect on the current state of affairs. The first scenario may materialize if the Koutla opposition agrees, and is allowed to form and lead a coalition government which will be empowered to bring about some tangible and positive change in the lives of most Moroccans. This would be possible if the USFP can muster and maintain support in both houses, not only from fellow Koutla partners but also from parties of the center bloc, especially the RNI, which has been preaching change and a break from past practices. Moreover, the entrance of the Islamists in parliament may contribute to a new tendency of inclusionary politics. This may help dampen the Islamist challenge that has exhibited its disruptive potential in the last few years, mainly on university campuses. To be a valid outlet and voice for the Islamist fervor, the parliament representatives of the MPDC and the al-Tawhid wa al-Islah movement would have to work very hard not only to be accepted among the political elite as a serious and respectable force, but also to convince the various Islamist currents in society that they can articulate their grievances and represent their views and interests.

The second scenario, that of the status quo, may prevail if the Koutla parties prove unable to form and sustain a relative cohesion among themselves and if a USFP-led coalition government cannot muster enough, and lasting, support within parliament and among the public at large. The status quo is likely to prevail also if the monarchy remains unwilling to share power and does not allow parliament to exercise its constitutional powers, or permit a new majority and a new government to be innovative in the public policy arena. In this case, Morocco will continue to present only a façade of democracy while its social contradictions and tensions continue to increase.

Notes

1. Remy Godeau, "Maroc: Recul de l'Opposition," *Jeune Afrique* 1707, September 23-29, 1993, p. 4.

2. Thomas C. Bayer, *Morocco: Direct Legislative Elections, June 25, 1993*, Report of the International Foundation for Electoral Systems (Washington, DC: IFES, 1993).

3. Source: Ibid.

4. "Al-Mou'aradha al-Maghribia Tou'aliqou al Amal 'ala Âoudati el-Faqih El-Basri," *Al-Hayat*, June 12, 1995, p. 6.

5. Source: *La Vie Economique*, a Moroccan weekly magazine, from various issues published from November 1997 to January 1998. Available on the Internet at: http://www.marocnet.net.ma/vieeco (especially, Issue 3925 of July 4-6, 1997). One hundred forty four municipalities fell under the control of smaller parties not included in Table 2.

6. This sentiment was publicly expressed by the leftist Parti de l'Avant-Garde Democratique (Party of Democratic Vanguarde, PADS), which called for a boycott of the municipal elections. Because of this call, 122 of its members were arrested and sentenced to jail terms and fines. Agence France Press, "Inculpation de 122 militants d'un parti d'opposition boycottant les elections," news dispatch, Rabat, June 8, 1997.

7. Source: Ministry of Communication, URL: www.mincom.gov.ma/ elections; *La Vie Economique*, Moroccan weekly magazine, several 1997-98 issues, URL: http://www.marocnet.net.ma/vieeco

IX

Prospects for Economic and Political Liberalization

Morocco's social and economic difficulties have deepened in recent years in spite of a major structural adjustment program. The unrest that shook several professions and universities in the last two years points to the urgent need for assertive state action to alleviate the social and economic malaise. However, can this be done without meaningful and inclusive political change? Up to now, the combination of an inhibited civil society and a persistent policy of exclusion has kept Morocco away from the political liberalization that was expected to accompany the economic reforms launched in 1983. However, it cannot be said that no progress at all has been made in decreasing the overwhelming weight of the state and the monarch on the political and economic spheres. Several measures were taken, including: economic liberalization; the abrogation of the 1935 *Dahir* on detention which did not adhere to universal principles of due process; the freeing of political prisoners in 1994; the 1996 parliamentary reform; the generally uncontested 1997 municipal and legislative elections; and the appointment of an opposition leader as prime minister. While there is some reason to be optimistic about the future, it may also be appropriate to be concerned about the slow pace of political reform and the social impact of the structural adjustment program.

Because economic restructuring requires efficiency and tightening of state spending, unemployment is likely to rise from the current 20 or 30 percent in the urban centers, and public expenditures on social services will continue to decrease as the state retreats further from many activities. Moreover, as the population continues to grow at a 2 percent rate per year, the number of new job-seekers will increase faster than job availability (60 percent of the population is below age 25), and the gap between rich and poor is likely to continue to widen. Until these problems are addressed and their solutions incorporated in the economic restructuring, they will continue to be a political liability that could threaten peace and stability, be it under King Hassan II or under his designated successor, Prince Sidi Mohamed.

In the last two decades, economic liberalization was given full attention not only because of international constraints and strong domestic pressures stemming from the failure of the public sector, but also as a result of pressures for privatization coming from big business in Morocco. However, political liberalization has come at a much slower pace. The relative lessening of control over the press and the recent elections and institutional reforms constitute important undertakings but it remains to be seen whether or not the monarch is truly ready to share power with a strengthened and increasingly independently-minded parliament and a former opposition leader turned prime minister.

In light of recent developments in Algeria and Tunisia, if a meaningful political change does not materialize in Morocco in the near future, the Islamists may effectively mobilize disaffected segments of society to increase pressure on the king to further open the political system—as has happened in Algeria—and to relinquish the monopoly he claims on both power and religion. In his *Le Monde Diplomatique* article of May 1996, Abderrahim Lamchichi outlined the recent evolution of the Islamist movement in Morocco and indicated that this movement has become prevalent in various sectors and among many segments of society. He concluded that

> the activist movements which call for the use of violence have disappeared or remained clandestine. Yet, small [violent] groups exist, as witnessed by their assistance to the Algerian GIA [Armed Islamic Group] and AIS [Army of Islamic Salvation]. In fact, these young militants, frustrated by a socio-economic system that excludes them, will not hesitate, at the right time, to take action. Their actions, often very radical and violent, already occurred in recent times (in January 1979 in protest against the presence of the Shah of Iran in Morocco; in March 1979 against the Camp David Accords; in 1990 during the Gulf War; in January 1981, January 1984, December 1990, etc.).[1]

In fact, in 1996, the Islamists increased their activism and even dared to publicly demand the right to form a political party and the release of Abdesslam Yacine from house arrest. These demands were expressed during a December 1996 university strike (which involved sit-ins and hunger strikes) in Casablanca. The state responded with repression and jail terms.

A wide societal mobilization by radical Islamists may become reality in Morocco if the current economic difficulties lead to a general crisis in which the gap between rich and poor widens, if the traditional opposition remains unable to effectively challenge failing economic and social policies, and if the secularization of society continues its advance, as happened elsewhere in the Maghrib and the Mashriq. Urbanization, secular education, the communication of western values through the media, and the weakening of the values of the large family, have been pushing Moroccan society slowly but surely toward greater secularization. This secularization provides the Islamists with the same tools that their counterparts in Algeria, Tunisia, and Egypt (and Iran in 1978-79) have used to challenge the regimes of their respective countries and to mobilize large segments of the population for a political rebellion under the banner of Islam.

Another potential threat to the regime's stability is the military. When the issue of the Western Sahara is resolved—either through the planned UN-organized referendum or by other means—the demobilization of the army may cause a serious concern. "No matter what the outcome of the Western Sahara conflict, the problem of reintegration of the army in society will have an impact on the equilibrium of the system which will need to mobilize new resources in order to continue satisfying its demands, unless, after the Sahara, it becomes engaged in an eventual re-conquest of the Presides."[2]

In order to preempt some of these potential negative developments and deal effectively with the social and economic challenges facing Morocco today, the monarchy may find it more in its interest to share power now with a "tolerable" opposition rather than face an unwanted and radical one in the future. It may also be advantageous to allow an independent and effective associative life—not to say civil society—to flourish and to counterbalance a potentially challenging partisan opposition in parliament and in government.

Notes

1. Abderrahim Lamchichi, "Les incertitudes politiques et sociales: L'islamism s'enracine au Maroc," *Le Monde Diplomatique*, May 1996, pp. 10-11.

2. Jean-Claude Santucci, "Etat et Société au Maroc: Enjeux et Perspectives du Changement," in Jean-Claude Santucci, ed., *Le Maroc Actuel: Une Modernisation au Miroir de la Tradition?* (Paris: CNRS, 1992, p. 431. (Translation mine.)

Conclusion

In Morocco, where the boundaries between state and society are blurred by strong institutional practices and by cultural and religious beliefs, perennial multiparty politics and associative life have neither generated a pluralist and democratic process nor stimulated the development of a civil society as defined early in this book. In the current circumstances of Morocco, the empirical significance and analytical usefulness of the notion of civil society are severely limited by many factors, including:

❖ The configuration of political life itself, which rests heavily on the centrality and "unchallengeability" of a king who dominates most spheres of Moroccan society (political, economic, civil, cultural, and religious). This configuration has constituted a major obstacle to the birth and development of independent social forces (i.e., elements of a civil society) that may peacefully and democratically question the nature of the existing system and even the king's monopoly over it;

❖ The persistent existence of the informal structures of the *makhzen* which prevent the rationalization of political interaction through modern institutions and processes;

❖ Public policies and laws that continue to inhibit the independent mobilization of differentiated societal interests;

❖ The very close identification of most members of the political elite with the state. This identification will continue as long as it remains a source of personal prestige and privilege.

Morocco stands today at a major crossroads, notably because of the expected succession of Sidi Mohamed to the throne and also because mounting domestic contradictions and increasing international pressures urgently require major policy shifts in order to avoid a general breakdown. At this crossroads, Morocco faces two possible alternatives: to engage in an effective political liberalization, or to maintain the status quo in the face of a society yearning for substantial change. Both alternatives carry political risks, and the question for the monarch is which one carries the lesser risk and the highest return in the long run.

Morocco has the potential to become the second example in the Arab world—after that of Jordan—of peacefully moving toward genuine political openness. However, it also has the potential to experience long-term social and political instability as a result of the combined negative effects of economic liberalization and political stagnation. To minimize this risk, the monarchy may find it useful to open up the political system so that it not only shares power with the opposition but also makes that opposition share the blame for inadequate public policies.

For a peaceful transition to an open polity to take place, state-society relations must be seriously reexamined and redefined. A genuine political liberalization would allow independently mobilized social and economic forces to play an active role in the process of deciding "who gets what, when, and how" in Morocco. Some of the factors that can help a smooth transition to a democratic setting already exist in Morocco. They include a long experience with associative life; established—albeit controlled—multiparty politics; a growing educated urban middle class; and international and regional conditions which carry strong pressures and incentives for positive change. This transition may be aided by a recently developed political language in Morocco which includes notions such as democracy, civil society, and pluralism. Even though these notions have yet to become fully operational in Morocco, they may be effectively manipulated by parties and associations to prompt a genuine political opening which progressively enlarges the limited space of freedoms allowed by the political regime.

However, the danger of regression toward absolute authoritarianism is still present; the relative opening of recent years remains fragile and is not yet fully institutionalized. The factors that may prompt a return to strict authoritarianism include the fear among some elements of the power establishment that a full political opening may mean a loss of control over the social, economic, and political situation and a loss of the privileges associated with the existing regime. This fear was illustrated by the governmental response to the Islamist mobilization in the universities of Casablanca, Marrakesh, and Mohammedia in the winter of 1996-97. The government responded with repression; many of the arrested students were members of the Islamist association al-'Adl wa al-Ihsan.[1] This event, like similar ones in the past, illustrates not only the limited space of political expression for some segments of society, but also the quick and uncompromising response of the state to societal challenges. The risk of a regression toward absolute authoritarianism may also increase if international pressures for democratization—as a condition for continued economic assistance and for a privileged association with the European Union—diminish. These pressures already started fading by the mid-1990s because some Western governments—especially France and the United States—feared that the Algerian crisis might prove contagious and threaten the stability of Morocco.[2]

In the Algerian case, the Islamists took advantage of a radical political liberalization in 1989 in the wake of major social upheaval in October 1988. The Islamists were allowed to organize and to mobilize people behind the explicit goals of getting rid of the existing regime and establishing an Islamic republic under their control. By the time the regime in place reacted to the mounting power of the Islamist movement, it was too late. The Islamists, led by the Islamic Salvation Front (FIS), won a landslide victory in the first round of the 1991 parliamentary elections; when the military intervened to cancel the vote in January 1992, the movement had already become uncontrollable and began an armed rebellion against the state and civilians suspected of collaborating with the regime or of simply refusing to aid the rebellion. Between 1992 and 1998, nearly 100,000 people were killed in this strife, which is not likely to end soon. In the meantime, the Algerian government drastically curtailed the democratization process and, in the name of fighting armed Islamist groups, engaged in a harsh repression, effectively closing the political space it had previously opened.

In Tunisia, too, President Zine al-Abidine Ben Ali shelved in 1989 his earlier promises of political pluralism by instituting total control over the state and society by his party, the Rassemblement Constitutionnel Démocratique (Constitutional Democratic Rally, RCD). In the parliamentary elections of 1994 only 19 seats were given to non-RCD deputies, and in the municipal elections, of 4,000 seats, only 6 were allocated to opposition candidates. Here too, the inhibition of an incipient political pluralism was justified by a threat perceived to come from radical Islamist groups.[3] Yet, in spite of this closing of the political sphere, and various reports of human rights abuses in Tunisia, Western governments—mainly France and the United States—have not been terribly concerned by the increasing level of repression and the diminishing respect for political freedoms in Tunisia. They expressed great satisfaction with the ongoing economic liberalization and with political stability, while publicly ignoring the authoritarian nature of the Tunisian regime.[4]

A similar evolution may occur in the case of Morocco: a return to absolute monarchy may no longer be a concern to the West as long as economic liberalization continues and as long as radical opposition (Islamist and other) is kept in check. The problem here is not the inhibition of radical opposition itself—this is practiced in all countries and by all regimes—but the effect of such policies on moderate and usually tolerated opposition. In other words, a regression in political openness due to threats posed by radicals may very well translate into a muzzling of all moderate political and social forces—just as has happened in Algeria and Tunisia after the mid-1990s.

The Moroccan monarchy may still manage to steer away from the Algerian and Tunisian experiences by allowing the development of a civic culture and independent organizations representing various social, economic, and cultural interests. The multiple restrictions currently imposed on the development of such societal structures need to be relaxed progressively not only to permit associations and parties to participate more freely in the development debate, but also to avoid the violent polarization that modernization and economic crisis may generate. In sum, to be able to manage adequately the important social and economic changes that Morocco is experiencing today, economic liberalization must be paired with political liberalization. Otherwise, it may become difficult to reconcile economic liberalization with a highly centralized political order.[5]

The development of a genuine and effective civil society in Morocco is difficult today because of the nature of the political system itself and the resistance of the political elite. In such a system, and short of clever innovation by the king himself, no substantial initiatives are expected from established opposition groups and leaders. In the absence of such initiatives from the king and/or the political elite, a serious push for change may then come from either new and young forces—be they Islamist or leftist—that have no stake in the existing system, or from the army after the Western Sahara issue is resolved.

In a discussion with John Waterbury in the mid-1990s, I mentioned that, while re-reading his twenty-eight-year-old book on Morocco, *The Commander of the Faithful*, I was struck by the fact that many of his observations were still very valid today. His only reaction was: "It's scary!" As the following excerpt from Waterbury's 1970 book demonstrates, Moroccan political life seems to have been frozen in time, and a peaceful transition to an open polity in which there is room for a civil society remains even today a remote possibility:

> The king strives to remain the sole Moroccan with a following, influence, and authority in both camps [the mountains and the urban centers].... [T]he educated urban bourgeoisie, the politicians, bureaucrats, and merchants are unable to exercise any positive role in the evolution of the regime. They are once again victims of fundamental political and social divisions that are kept in precarious equilibrium, and while they would like to mitigate these divisions and bring about a re-ordering of Moroccan society within an explicitly nationalist framework, they shy away from the positive actions for fear of the upheaval their endeavors would entail. The monarchy is a marvelous excuse for the Moroccan elite to benefit from a system that it refuses to espouse and for whose shortcomings it shirks all responsibility. The king realizes that the perfunctory grumblings of his clientele will most probably never take the form of an overt challenge to his regime upon whose rewards the elite has come to depend. Inescapably, new elites, with little or no stake in the present but great hopes in the future, will take up the responsibilities their elders have refused to assume.[6]

The paradox of Waterbury's remark is that while his observations are still valid, the hopeful prediction in his last sentence has failed to materialize. King Hassan II has cleverly averted a potential rupture with his society and the real opposition has not been able to muster enough momentum and strength to prompt change. Moreover, the Western Sahara crisis of the 1970s provided the king with an invaluable means to silence the opposition—both the tolerated and non-tolerated. But now that Morocco has imposed its *de facto* control over the "useful" part of the Western Sahara, the consensus around irredentism no longer serves as the basis for an overall agreement on other issues. This explains why, in recent years, opposition to the monarchy and the state over political and human rights issues has increased; it also explains why the king has made some concessions to the opposition—it is the only means to contain both domestic discontent and international pressures.

In the context of major international mutations and important social and economic changes at home, the Moroccan regime has been under strong external pressure to institute a political evolution which will project a favorable international image while enacting the smallest possible political opening at home. The regime undertook various actions in 1993 and 1994 to enhance Morocco's standing in international public opinion and in regional affairs, including hosting the last GATT meeting in Casablanca, the Middle East and North Africa economic conference—which welcomed a large Israeli delegation—and the establishment of low-level diplomatic relations with Israel. On the domestic front, various decisions were made to alleviate some pressure for political change. However, the political opening of recent years needs to move ahead; the entire political class could only gain from it. Rather than risk being seriously challenged by popular upheaval and losing everything, the regime may be better served by accommodating some of the new forces through inclusion in the policy-making process and by instituting accountability mechanisms. The appointment of Youssoufi as prime minister is certainly an important step in that direction, but a more comprehensive political opening should include effective empowerment of parliament and its government, decentralization of state power so as to lessen the control of the powerful Interior Ministry and its local offices, and increased freedom of expression—without threats of persecution. The regime should invite the Moroccan people to engage in associative life and provide them with the legal means and guarantees to do so. Through associative activities, people would be able to promote their various interests and protect themselves from the arbitrary uses of the powers of the state and its administrative agents. Of course, this "political equity" will only be real if it is accompanied by an economic equity based on a mix of market rules and traditional ethics of national solidarity.

The advancement of associative life for the purpose of a genuine and effective popular participation in the design of public policies does not necessarily mean a weakening of the state in the face of independently mobilized societal interests. As Western experiences show, a relatively strong state will always be needed. However, it is the arbitrary use of state power and the policies of exclusion that a participatory associative life would guard against. Civil society does not inevitably threaten the state. In fact, in theory and in practice, each is dependent on the other and each can strengthen and legitimize the other. Civil society, as an instrument of mediation between the state and society at large, needs the state since that is its *raison d'être*. If civil society were completely independent from the state, however, there would be two competing entities in all political, ideological, cultural, and economic spheres. Instead, civil society interacts with the state apparatus—which wields administrative capacity and the monopoly of force—for the purpose of affecting authoritative decisions in a symbiotic way; it mediates between societal wants and state whim. In an ideal scenario, the Moroccan monarchy and state would agree to limit their roles to regulating society equitably, providing services for the least fortunate segments of the population, and mediating between various groups (parties, associations, regional interests, etc.) which would constitute, some day, a civil society. The monarchy may then remain the ultimate symbol of national unity, while parties and associations would affect public policy directly and through political negotiations. Short of being co-opted, the socialist-led government of Youssoufi must find a way to move the country in that more democratic direction. It may be now the only option available to Morocco if it wishes to avoid the breakdown experienced elsewhere in the region.

Notes

1. Agence France Press, "Le gouvernement marocain part en guerre contre les étudiants islamistes," news dispatch, Rabat, January 20, 1997; Agence France Press, "La classe politique marocaine s'interroge sur les mouvements islamistes," news dispatch, Rabat, January 31, 1997.

2. According to official accounts, the August 1994 Islamist attack in Marrakesh was perpetrated by an Algerian-Moroccan Islamist network that planned to destabilize Morocco. This event stimulated strong police actions that sought to neutralize people suspected of posing a domestic threat.

3. Ahmed Ibrahimi (pseudonym), "Les liberties envolées de la Tunisie," *Le Monde Diplomatique*, February, 1997, pp. 4-5.

4. During their visits to Tunisia in 1995, French President Jacques Chirac and US Under Secretary of State for Middle East Affairs Robert Pelletreau Jr. focused their public statements mostly on the economic progress made by Tunisia, while hardly acknowledging the human rights concerns raised by various international organizations.

5. Abed Darwisha, "Reasons for Resilience," in Abed Darwisha and I. William Zartman, eds., *Beyond Coercion: The Durability of the Arab State* (New York: Croom Helm, 1988), p. 280.

6. John Waterbury, *The Commander of the Faithful*, (New York, NY: Columbia University Press, 1970), p. 315.

APPENDIX

Partial List of Political Parties and Civic Associations

Political Parties

Action Populaire al-Ansar (APA)
Constitutional Union (UC)
Democratic Party of Independents (PDI)
Front of Democratic Forces (FFD)
Istiqlal Party (PI)
National Rally of Independents (RNI)
National Union of Popular Forces (UNFP)
National Popular Movement (MNP)
National Democratic Party (PND)
Organization of Democratic and Popular Action (OADP)
Party of Action (PA)
Party of Progress and Socialism (PPS)
Popular Democratic and Constitutional Movement (MPDC)
Popular Movement (MP)
Socialist Democratic Party (PSD)
Socialist Union of Popular Forces (USFP)

Women's Associations

Association of Protection of the Moroccan Family
Association of Women in Legal Careers
Committee of Moroccan Women for Development
Democratic Association of Moroccan Women
Democratic League For the Rights of the Woman
Federation of Women in Liberal and Commercial Careers
Moroccan Association "Espace Point De Depart" for the Promotion of
    the Feminine Enterprise
National Association of Female Cadres of Public and Semi-Public
    Administrations
National League of Women Functionaries in the Public and Private Sectors
National Organization of the Democratic Woman

National Union of Moroccan Women
Organization of the Istiqlalian Women
Union of Feminine Action
Moroccan Association of Family Planning

Business Associations

Association of Mining Industries of Morocco (AIMM)
General Moroccan Economic Confederation (CGEM)
Federation of Canning Industries of Morocco
Federation of Chemical Industries (FIC)
Federation of Industries of Fat Products
Federation of Travel Agents of Morocco
Moroccan Agricultural Union
Moroccan Association for Automobile Industry and Commerce
    (AMICA)
Moroccan Association of Exporters (ASMEX)
Moroccan Association of Flower Producer-Exporters (AMPEXFLEURS)
Moroccan Association of Publishers
Moroccan Association of the Textile Industry
Moroccan Association of Citrus Fruit Producers
National Federation of Hotel Industry (FNIH)
Moroccan Federation of Insurance Companies
National Federation of Insurance Agents and Brokers of Morocco
    (FNACAM)
Moroccan Federation of Leather Industries ((FEDIC)
Professional Association of Materials Importers
Professional Committee of Moroccan Mills

Religious Associations

al-'Adl wa al-Ihsan
al-Jama'a al-Islamiyya
al-Rabita
al-Tabligh Oual-Da'awa Lillah
Jama'at al-Tabligh wa al-Da'wa
Jam'iyyat al-Shabiba al-Islamiyya
Harakat al-Mujahidin
Harakat al-Tawhid wa al-Islah

Labor Unions

Association of Moroccan Workers (SNP)
Federation of Popular Unions (USP)
General Union of Moroccan Workers (UGTM)
Labor Union of Free Workers (USTL)
Moroccan Labor Forces (MLF)
Moroccan Labor Union (MTU)
Moroccan Workers Union (UTM)
National Popular Union (NPU)
National Union of Moroccan Workers (UNTM)
Union of Free Worker's Association (FOM)
Workers' Democratic Confederation (CDT)

Environmental Associations

Association for the Fight Against Erosion and Desertification
(ALCESDAM)
Association for the Protection and Improvement of Plant Life
(ANAPPAV)
Moroccan Association for the Promotion of Renewable Energies
(AMPER)
Moroccan Association for the Protection of the Environment
(ASMAPE)
Moroccan Ecological Association
Moroccan Society for Environmental Law (SOMADE)
National Association for Land Improvement, Irrigation and
Drainage (ANAFID)
National Movement of Moroccan Ecologists
Society for the Protection of Animals

Health Associations

Association of Parents and Friends of Children with Cancer (L'Avenir)
Moroccan Association of Deaf Children
Moroccan Association for the Fight Against AIDS (ALCS)
Moroccan Association of Hemophiliacs
Moroccan Association of Support and Assistance to Children with
Language Disability (AMESDL)

Moroccan League of the Fight Against Sexually Transmitted Diseases
Organization Alawite (for assistance to the handicapped)
Organization of the Moroccan Red Crescent

Youth and Student Associations

Association of Unemployed Graduates
General Union of Moroccan Students (UGEM)
Moroccan Federation of Associations of Work Camps
National Council of Youth and the Future (CNJA)
National Union of Moroccan Students (UNEM)
Youth of the Party of Progress and Socialism (JPPS)

Human Rights Associations

Association for the Defense of Human Rights in Morocco
    (ASDHOM, France)
Committee for the Defense of Human Rights
Moroccan Bar Association
Moroccan Human Rights Association
Moroccan League of Human Rights (LMDH)
Moroccan Organization for Human Rights (OMDH)

Amazigh (Berber) Associations

Association Assala
Association Bine al Ouidane
Association of the Mediterranean Basin
Association Tellili
Cultural Association of Soussa
Moroccan Association for Research and Cultural Exchange (AMREC)

Regional Cultural Associations (Government-sponsored)

Association Ahmed al-Hansali
Association Angad al-Maghreb al-Sharqi
Association Bouregreg
Association Chaouia
Association of Doukkala
Association Fes-Saiss

Association du Grand Atlas
Association La Grande Ismailia
Association Hawd-Assafi
Association Illigh
Association Jbel Al-ayachi
Association al-Mouhit
Association al Nahda-Nador
Association Ribat Al Fath
Association Sidi Mohamed Ben Abdellah
Association Tetouan Smir
Association l'Unite du Bassin De Sebou

International Non-Governmental Organizations

Catholic Relief Services (CRS)
Comité d'Entraide International (CEI)
Save the Children
Terre des Hommes

Index

Chamber of Labor Unions: 83
Charter of Human Rights: 56
civil society: viii–ix, 11, 13–15, 41, 75; definitions: 11, 39–40; development of: 41–45, 101; obstacles to: 41
Claisse, Alain: 30
clientelism: 29
Code of Personal Status (*Mudawana*): 52, 60, 63
Comité d'Entraide International (CEI): 67
Committee for the Defense of Human Rights: 56
communal councils: 83
concept of citizen: 41. *See also* Jamai, Khalid
Confederation of Labor: 23
constitution: 28–30, 83; Article 9: 43–45
Constitutional Reform, 1996: 83, 87-88
Constitutional Union (UC): 79, 94; parliamentary elections: 84
Consultative Council on Human Rights: 56
Cooperative associations for women: 61
Council of Ulama: 52
coup attempts: 32
Cultural Association of Soussa: 57

D

Dahir (Royal Decree), 1958: 40–41, 43–45;
Dahir of 1973: 43; Déclaration Préalable: 43
Da'wa (preaching associations): 52
de Tocqueville, Alexis: vii, 14
debt relief agreements: 21
debt servicing: 36
Democratic and Social Movement (MDS): 80, 88, 94
Democratic Association of Moroccan Women: 62
Democratic Labor Confederation (CDT): 49

Democratic Party of Independents (PDI): 80
democratization: viii, 15–16, 28, 42, 75
demographics: 24
Djama'a associations: 40
Doukkala cultural association: 48

E

Eastern Europe: 11, 36
economic liberalization: 28, 97, 102, 104
economics: 19–25, 44, 97; international aspects: 36–37
Egypt: vii, 15, 54, 99
El Benna, Abdelkader: 76
El-Yazghi, Mohamed: 86
elections, 1993: 30, 38, 62, 83-87; women candidates: 62; 1997: 30, 38, 90; Islamists: 93. *See also* municipal elections, parliamentary elections
emigrant workforce: 19
Engels, Friedrich: 12, 14
Environmental associations: 64
Europe: 22, 35
European Community: 36
European Economic Union (EEC): 23
European Union (EU): 22–23, 103

F

Federation of Canning Industries: 49
Federation of Industries of Fat Products: 49
Federation of Popular Unions: 50
Federation of Women in Liberal and Commercial Care: 61
Feminist associations: 60–63
Fez: 25, 47, 54, 77
Filali, Abdellatif: 58, 87, 92
foyers (women's aid centers): 59
France: 23, 56, 77, 86, 104
free-trade zone: 23
Front of Democratic Forces (FFD): 93